98

D0860264

WITHDRAWN

THE BOOK of DURROW

THE BOOK of DURROW

A medieval masterpiece at
Trinity College Dublin

Bernard Meehan

ROBERTS
RINEHART

TOWN HOUSE
DUBLIN

Published in Ireland by Town House and Country House
Trinity House, Charleston Road, Ranelagh, Dublin 6

ISBNs: 1-86059-005-5 (Hbk); 1-86059-006-3 (Pbk)

Published in the US and Canada by Roberts Rinehart
Publishers, 5455 Spine Road, Boulder, Colorado 80301
Distributed by Publishers Group West

ISBN: 1-57098-053-5 (Hbk)

British Library Cataloguing in Publication Data. A catalogue
record for this book is available from the British Library.

Library of Congress Catalog Card No. 95-74900

Acknowledgements
The author is indebted to the following for advice and
comment: Jane Maxwell, Dr Dáibhí Ó Cróinín, Felicity
O'Mahony, William O'Sullivan, Dr Michael Ryan, Susan M
Youngs, Dr Niamh Whitfield (for generous advice on parallels
with jewellery and for some valuable references). Thanks are
due also to Mrs Margaret E Bruce-Mitford for sight of an
unpublished study of the Book of Durrow by the late Dr
Rupert Bruce-Mitford.

The author and publishers would like to thank the following
for permission to reproduce photographs: The Green Studio
Ltd (p8); National Museum of Ireland (pp11, 50, 70);
Biblioteca Nazionale Universitaria, Turin (p20); Dean and
Chapter Library, The College, Durham (p23), Royal Irish
Academy, Dublin (p28); University Museum of National
Antiquities, Oslo, Norway (p35); Board of Trinity College
Dublin (pp36, 54, and all pages from the Book of Durrow);
Bibliothèque Nationale, Paris (pp41, 63); Kunsthal,
Rotterdam (p43); Hunt Museum, Limerick (p46); Chester
Beatty Library, Dublin (p47); British Museum (pp71, 73).

Cover: Book of Durrow, folio 84v

Designed by Wendy Williams
Printed in Hong Kong by Colorcorp/Sing Cheong

For MSL

Contents

INTRODUCTION

THE BOOK OF DURROW contains an early medieval manuscript copy of the four Gospels, along with certain preliminary matter. Now containing 248 folios, measuring c 245 x 145 mm (c $9^{1}/2$ x $5^{1}/2$ ins), it is written in a superb Irish majuscule script, accompanied by pages of ornament by an artist who produced some of the most striking images in insular art.[1] In aspects of its background, decoration and preliminary texts — though not its Gospel texts — it is closely related to the Book of Kells. It is most commonly dated to the late seventh century — more than a century before the Book of Kells — and, if written then, is the earliest surviving fully decorated insular Gospel manuscript. Its dating and origin have aroused fervent academic debate for much of the present century, while its sources, influences and iconography have provided scope for numerous comparative studies.

Both the extent of its decoration and the sophistication of its execution point strongly to the view that Durrow was not the first such manuscript produced. Any discussion of the insular manuscripts should bear in mind that surviving books form a slim residue of what once existed. The sources available to the artists are necessarily opaque because of such losses, while chance archaeological discoveries or fresh evaluations of individual manuscripts can alter substantially our perceptions of the period. For this reason, it is occasionally necessary to draw on parallels which are remote in time or place, but which may themselves have drawn on sources common to insular artists. It is difficult to discuss the Book of Durrow in isolation, since knowledge of its art and texts depends to a great extent on comparisons with contemporary metalwork and with other manuscripts, but most surviving insular manuscripts cannot be dated or located with sufficient precision to allow the establishment of a relative chronology.

OPPOSITE:
High cross of Durrow,
County Offaly
(The Green Studio Ltd)

BACKGROUND

THE TRADITIONAL ASSOCIATION of the Book of Durrow is with the monastery of Durrow, County Offaly, about six kilometres (four miles) north of Tullamore, founded by St Colum Cille. Born in Donegal *c* 521 into the Cenél Conaill branch of the Uí Néill, Colum Cille traced a direct descent from Niall of the Nine Hostages, founder of the family. In 563 he left Ireland along with twelve followers for the west coast of Scotland, 'wishing to be a pilgrim for Christ', as his biographer Adomnán informs us.[2] Colum Cille became head of a large confederation of monastic houses, including Derry, in the north of Ireland, which he may have founded before leaving Ireland, and Iona, a small island to the west of Mull, off the Scottish coast, which became his principal house, and where he died in 597. Iona acted as a great missionary centre both in Colum Cille's time and later. It was from here that St Aidan travelled to Northumbria in the north of England to found the monastery of Lindisfarne in 635.

It is not clear precisely when Colum Cille's monastery at Durrow was founded. It is believed that the site was given by Aíd, son of Brénnan, king of the southern Uí Néill kingdom of Tethbe, who died in 589, but it is not known if this was before or after Colum Cille left Ireland. Writing in the eighth century, Bede informs us that before he left Ireland, Colum Cille 'had founded a famous monastery (*monasterium nobile*) in Ireland called Dearmach (Durrow), the Field of the Oaks, on account of the great number of oaks there'.[3] It may however be inferred from Adomnán that the foundation of Durrow took place while Colum Cille was on a visit from Iona sometime after 585. Adomnán tells of an incident that occurred during a period 'when for some months the blessed man remained in the midland district of Ireland, while by God's will founding the monastery that is called in Irish *Dairmag* [Durrow]'. At this time Colum Cille visited Clonmacnoise, also in County Offaly, where he was treated with all the reverence due to an

Enamel mount, probably eighth-century, from Lough Derravaragh, County Westmeath *(National Museum of Ireland, E 499: 325)*

OPPOSITE:
Book of Durrow
folio 1v

elder saint, 'senior sanctus'. The phrase may be a conventional one and need not imply that he was elderly and so visiting from Iona. It is known from Adomnán that building was in progress on Durrow while Colum Cille was on Iona. One cold winter's day, Colum Cille wept at the knowledge that Laisráin, presumably the abbot, 'is now harassing my monks in the construction of a large building, although they are exhausted with heavy labour'. At that point, Laisráin, 'as if kindled with an inner fire, ordered that the monks should cease work'. It may have been during the same building programme that one of the community fell from the top of the round monastic house at Durrow. The incident was perceived by Colum Cille as he sat writing in his hut on Iona, and an angel was dispatched to catch the monk before he hit the ground.

Other stray references to the founder's concern for Durrow occur in Adomnán's *Life*. On one occasion, for example, Colum Cille was able miraculously to improve the flavour of fruit from a tree near Durrow that cropped abundantly, but bore fruit that was 'more hurtful than pleasing to those that tasted it'.[4]

Little information is available about Durrow in the Middle Ages, a situation that may be attributed at least in part to the loss of its library late in the eleventh century. The Annals of Ulster record for the year 1095 the burning of many churches, among them 'Durrow with its books'. That it was prominent in its early years may however be judged from Bede's remark that 'From both of these [that is, Iona and Durrow] sprang very many monasteries which were established by his disciples in Britain and Ireland, over all of which the island monastery in which his body lies held pré-eminence'.[5] Regrettably, Bede did not provide details of Durrow's daughter foundations. The survival of one elaborate high cross, standing over three metres (ten feet) high, carved with scenes from the Old and New Testaments, testifies to the wealth and stability of the monastery in the ninth century, when it was probably erected.[6]

History
of the
Manuscript

THE MANUSCRIPT IS FIRST LOCATED with certainty in Durrow in the period between 877 and 916, when Flann Mac Mael Sechnaill, king of Ireland, placed it in a *cumdach* (shrine), believing it to be a relic of St Colum Cille. The impact damage, which can be observed at the beginning and end of the book and at its edges, may be attributed to a large extent to the ill-fitting nature of the shrine. Another aspect of its enshrinement was probably that it was no longer in use as a book, since most shrines seem to have been constructed so as not to allow ready access. Flann's son Donnchadh, incidentally, had a shrine made for the Book of Armagh in 937, believing it to be the work of St Patrick. The Durrow shrine was lost during the period of military occupation of Trinity College in 1689, the book being left with only 'a plain brown rough leathern cover', as Narcissus Marsh, then archbishop of Dublin, described it in 1699. The shrine's existence is known from the record of the antiquary Roderick O'Flaherty, who saw it in 1677 and recorded, in a note that now forms folio IIv of the manuscript, that it was adorned with a silver cross. On one arm of the cross the name of the craftsman was recorded in an inscription in Irish — though O'Flaherty did not transcribe it — while along the length of the cross was an inscription invoking the blessing of St Colum Cille on King Flann, who caused the shrine to be made.[7] Little is known otherwise about the book in the Middle Ages. While it may be possible to identify it as one of the two Gospel books which the Annals of Tigernach records were taken to Kells from Donegal among the relics of St Colum Cille in 1090,[8] it was certainly at Durrow in the late eleventh or early twelfth century, as is known from a *notitia* or *aide-mémoire* on folio 248v, which records the ceding to the monastery of Durrow of land belonging to the monastery of Glenn Uissen in County Carlow.[9]

After the dissolution of the monastery of Durrow in the mid-sixteenth century, the precise whereabouts of the manuscript are not known with certainty. James Ussher, archbishop of Armagh, carefully collated its Gospel text with the same text in the Book of Kells, as he describes in *Britannicarum Ecclesiarum Antiquitates* (1639). This work was probably done, or at least initiated, while Ussher was bishop of Meath between 1621 and 1623.[10]

It is clear from a note made by Michael O'Clery around the year 1630 that the manuscript, which remained in local hands, was still revered as the Book of Colum Cille.[11] It was a commonplace of medieval hagiography that a book written by a saint was impervious to immersion in water. Adomnán used this device in describing miracles associated with St Colum Cille.[12] In a translation of the Annals of Clonmacnoise, completed in 1627, Connall MacEochagáin of Lismoyne, County Westmeath, recorded that the custodian in his time of the Book of Durrow dipped it in water and gave the water to sick cattle as a cure:

> [St Colum Cille's] bookes have a strange property which is that if they or any of them had sunk to the bottom of the deepest waters they would not lose one letter, signe, or character of them, wch I have seen partly myselfe of that book of them which is at Dorow in the Ks County, for I saw the Ignorant man that had same in his Custody, when sickness came upon cattle, for their Remedy putt water on the booke & suffered it to rest there a while & saw alsoe cattle return thereby to their former or pristin state & the book to receave no loss.[13]

It seems that only a section of the book was used for this purpose, the present folios 208 to 221 from the Gospel of St John (6.63–12.4), a section of fourteen leaves of what originally were conjoint bifolia, the largest section of the book. A hole in the top right corner prompted the suggestion that a

OPPOSITE:
Book of Durrow
folio 2r

string was run through the leaves and the section hung on a nail when not in use. These leaves show particular signs of water damage, there is considerable depletion of ink, and the vellum has become quite translucent.[14]

The book's custody passed to Henry Jones, who presented it, and the Book of Kells, to Trinity College (the University of Dublin) in the period he served as bishop of Meath, from 1661 to 1682. A graduate of the college in 1621, and bishop of Clogher from 1645, Jones had served as scoutmaster general to Cromwell's army in Ireland, and was vice-chancellor of the university from 1646 to 1660. In 1681 Jones informed William Palliser, then professor of divinity at Trinity College, that the Books of Kells and Durrow were to be identified with the Gospel manuscripts studied by Ussher. The Book of Durrow at that time had no catalogue number or shelf-mark, being known only as 'the Cupboard MS', stored there presumably because of the value of the shrine.[15]

DATING *and* ORIGIN

THERE HAS BEEN prolonged debate over where and when the Book of Durrow was written. Up to the 1930s, its provenance meant that it was regarded unquestioningly as having originated in Durrow, even if some nineteenth-century scholars like J O Westwood were sceptical of its attribution to the hand of St Colum Cille. For A W Clapham (1934), however, the great Gospel books of Kells and Durrow, and their close relations, the Lindisfarne and Durham Gospels, were the result of a cultural process which took place in Northumbria rather than in Ireland, since 'The Irish came to Northumbria without any form of Celtic art-expression, and left it capable of producing the highest forms of Irish Christian art'.[16] The discovery of the ship burial at Sutton Hoo in Suffolk in the late 1930s was taken to support a Northumbrian origin for Durrow, due to striking parallels between some of the objects found there and motifs used in the manuscript.[17] In his great corpus of manuscripts dating from before 800, E A Lowe remarked, in a passage often quoted, 'I confess that the Book of Durrow has always seemed to me a book apart among the group of early Irish manuscripts now at Dublin, and gradually the suspicion woke in me that perhaps English workmanship accounted for the orderliness of its script and the balance and sobriety of its ornamentation'. He concluded that Durrow was produced 'in Northumbria by a hand trained in the Irish manner'.[18] The Swedish scholar Carl Nordenfalk found himself broadly in

agreement with this view.[19] François Masai followed the same path in an influential study published in 1947: *'Essai sur les origines de la miniature dite irlandaise.'* As his title suggests, Masai found no role for Irish inspiration in the art of the period. It may be noted that because he was working from the confines of a Belgian prison during the War, Masai did not actually see the Book of Durrow. Julian Brown supported Masai in a series of publications, particularly in a controversial paper focusing on the Book of Kells which he published in 1972.[20]

For those who regarded Durrow as a Northumbrian manuscript, it was necessary to use stylistic grounds to date it relative to other manuscripts seen as Northumbrian productions: the Lindisfarne Gospels (British Library, Cotton Nero D. IV), which may be dated in the period between 687 and 721, albeit on the basis of a colophon written three hundred years later, the Durham Gospels (Durham Dean and Chapter Library, A.II.17), and the Echternach Gospels (Paris, Bibliothèque Nationale, lat. 9389), which carry no precise dating criteria. Masai dated Durrow around the year 700. Lowe first placed it in the eighth, then in the second half of the seventh century,[21] while Nordenfalk opted for a date in the last third of the seventh century.[22] Julian Brown concluded that Lindisfarne was written *c* 698, with Durrow, which has more 'freedom' of script, at a point before then.[23]

The French archaeologist Françoise Henry consistently regarded Durrow as an Irish product, relating it to the cross at Carndonagh, County Donegal, and the slab at Fahan Mura, some thirty-two kilometres (twenty miles) distant, now generally dated to the eighth or ninth century. She suggested that the Columban monastery of Derry, close to these monuments, may have been where the manuscript was written, or at least decorated, since she regarded scribe and artist as distinct.[24] A A Luce also stressed the Columban background to and context of the Book of Durrow in his lengthy 1960 introduction to the facsimile of the manuscript, pointing out the key role that the Book of Durrow occupied for those who espoused the Northumbrian cause: 'an Irish Book of Durrow would tear the [Northumbrian] theory to flitters'.[25]

A re-examination of the manuscripts produced at the monastery of

OPPOSITE:
Book of Durrow
folio 3v

19

Echternach prompted Dáibhí Ó Cróinín to argue that their script may have been developed not in Northumbria, as Lowe, Brown and others had supposed, but in Ireland, specifically at Rath Melsigi, the monastery in County Carlow where, as Bede tells us, the English missionary Willibrord had spent several years before setting out on his continental mission in 690. Ó Cróinín has pointed to similarities between Durrow and the calendar of Willibrord in Paris (Bibliothèque Nationale, MS lat. 10837), which he can date to the first decade of the eighth century, in particular to a distinctive vertical flourish or divider common to Durrow folio 124r (p55) and the Willibrord calendar folio 30v. Ó Cróinín's view is that the book was made in Durrow and for Durrow. By inference, this took place in the first decade of the eighth century, if, as Ó Cróinín suggests, the scribe of the Willibrord calendar was also the scribe of the Augsburg Gospels (Universitätsbibliothek Augsburg, Cod. I.2.4°2), which he dates *c* 705.[26]

In 1987 George Henderson expressed a preference for Iona as the place where the Book of Durrow was produced, if a date of *c* 675 is accepted, but concluded that it would make sense as a Northumbrian production if its date were pushed back closer to the middle of the century.[27] Martin Werner concurred with an origin at Iona.[28]

William O'Sullivan has stressed that palaeographical and textual, as well as art-historical, criteria must be applied in dating manuscripts; that artistic style does not necessarily take a straight line of development; and that attempts to place a chronology on Durrow, the Durham Gospels, Lindisfarne and Echternach, based on a fixed date for only one of these (Lindisfarne), are false. He relates Durrow to the manuscripts produced at Echternach early in the eighth century, and to the script pages of Turin (Biblioteca Nazionale Universitaria, O.IV.20), a manuscript severely damaged by fire in 1904. Julian Brown had regarded the scripts of Durrow and Turin as the work of the same scribe, whereas O'Sullivan sees them as the product of training in the same scriptorium. Four decorated pages surviving from the Turin manuscript (two carpet pages, the Second Coming and the Ascension)[29] do not relate stylistically to Durrow, but O'Sullivan explains this difficulty in geographical terms 'as involving mobile scribes

Biblioteca Nazionale
Universitaria, Torino, MS
F.VI.2, fasc VIII, folio 1v

OPPOSITE:
Book of Durrow
folio 4r

NOUUM OPU[S]

facere me cogis ex
ueteri ut post exem
plaria scribara
rum toto orbe dispersa
quasi quidam arbiter sedeo
et quia inter se uariant quae
sint illa quae cum graeca con
sentiant ueritate decernam

Pius labor sed periculosa
praesumptio iudicare de cete
ris ipsum ab omnibus iudicandum:
senis mutare linguam et canescentem
mundum ad initia retrahere par
uulorum. Quis enim doctus pariter
uel indoctus cum in manus uolumen
adsumpserit et a saliua quam se
mel inbibit uiderit discrepare
quod lectitat non statim erumpat
in uocem me falsarium me clamans
esse sacrilegum quid ad eam adi
quid in ueteribus libris addens muta
ns

working in different scriptoria, with different but contemporary artists, who chose to employ different ranges of motifs'.[30]

It seems, as scholarly opinion retreats from the views of those enthusiastic for a Northumbrian origin, that the Book of Durrow should be placed, as traditionally assumed, firmly in a Columban milieu. The colophon on folio 247v *(p78)* can be accepted, almost at face value, as evidence of this. The evidence also suggests that the book should be dated early in the eighth rather than late in the seventh century, though it must be stressed that such fine tuning of uncertain dates cannot be definitive. The community at Durrow was a renowned establishment in the eyes of Bede and Adomnán, and was presumably in a position to produce a decorated Gospel book for its own use, drawing for inspiration on other manuscripts and on jewellery and metalwork, some of it native, some of it imported. Iona retains a claim on the grounds of Durrow's textual links with the Book of Kells, which was the work of that scriptorium. One possible scenario is that the Book of Durrow left Iona when that community moved after 807 to Kells, and that it went from there to Durrow.

TECHNIQUES
of
DECORATION

MOST OF DURROW'S decorative techniques were familiar to earlier insular artists. 'Diminuendo', a technique that involved forming the opening words of a text in decreasing sizes, was used in the psalter known as the Cathach (Dublin, Royal Irish Academy, 12.R.33), traditionally believed to have been written by St Colum Cille *(p28)*. Dotting around a letter is known first in an Irish context in the late sixth- or early seventh-century Gospel book termed Usserianus Primus (Trinity College Dublin, MS 55). Dotting in Durrow could be executed with extraordinary delicacy, as on the face of the Man on 21v *(pp34, 35)*. Where it appears in bands of letters, it has no obvious calligraphic function, and resembles stippling on the Ardagh Chalice *(p70)*. In its employment of trumpet and spiral devices, and its mimicking of enamel and glass work, Durrow's decoration bears a marked resemblance to metalwork and jewellery.

Interlace, developed from the broad ribbon style of the earliest insular example, Durham A.11.10 *(p20)*, dominates the carpet pages (that is, pages entirely of abstract decoration) and the symbols pages, but is used more sparingly in the initials pages. Durrow's interlace has sharp and clear definitions but is 'loosely woven', as Françoise Henry put it,[31] with individual strands changing colour, in a manner found in early Coptic art, such as the Glazier codex from the late fourth or early fifth century (New York, Pierpont Morgan Library, MS 67). In the borders surrounding the Man on

Fragmentary seventh-century
Gospel book,
Durham Cathedral Library,
MS A.II.10, folio 3v

23

xliii	iii	xii	clxviiii	cci	xcviii
lxi	x	xxvii	clxxvii	xciii	ci
lxxi	cii	clxvii	clxxvii	xcii	cii
lxxiii	xxxviii	cxxiii	clviiii	xciii	ccviiii
lxxiii	xxxviiii	lxxviii	clxviiii	xciiii	cxcviii
l	xlii	liii	cxc	ccii	cxcii
lxiii	xlv	iiii	cxcii	ccii	ccviii
lxii	xlv	xcviii	cxciii	cciii	cxci
lxiiii	xlvii	xxxvii	cxcii	ccvii	ccxxiiii
lxviii	xlvi	xcvii	cxciiii	cciiii	clii
lxviiii	xlvii	lxxviii	cxciiii	cxciii	cxcviiii
lxxi	xlvi	xxcviiii	cxcii	cxciiii	ccxc
lxvii	xlvi	xxcvii	cxxviii	xc	ccxci
lxxii	xlvii	cxxxvii	cxcviii	cxi	cxxvii
lxxiii	xlvii	xl	cci	cxci	ccviii
lxxiiii	xlviiii	lxxvii	cciii	cxiii	cclxx
lxxvii	liii	clxxvii	ccvi	cxvii	cxxvii
lxxviiii	xxxviii	lxxvii	cciii	cxcii	ccxcii
lxxx	xxx	xlviiii	cciiii	cxviii	ccxciii
lxxvii	liii	lxxviii	ccxiiii	cxcviiii	cclxi
lxxxii	liii	xc	ccxviiii	cxcviiii	cclxii
lxxxiii	liiii	lxxxvii	ccxxiii	cxc	ccxliii
lxxvii	liiii	cxvii	ccxxii	cxcviiii	ccxlii
lxxxvii	lv	cxviii	ccxvii	cxcviii	cxliii
lxxvii	lvi	lxxviii	ccxviiii	ccvii	ccxxviii
lxxviiii	cclii	cxxviii	ccxxviiii	ccxvii	cclvii
lxxxviii	cclii	cclii	ccxlii	ccxcvii	ccxxxviii
xcii	xl	lxxx	ccxlii	ccxcviii	ccxlviiii
xciii	lxxvii	ccxxiii	ccxliii	ccxciii	ccxlviii
xcviii	lxxvii	cclii	ccxliiii	cxliii	cclii
c iii	l	lxx	ccxlviiii	cxliii	cclii
cxviii	xcviii	xli	ccxlviiii	cxliii	cclvii
cxcii	xxciii	xlii	ccli	cxlvi	cclii
ccxl	xxxvii	xxcviii	ccxiii	cxlviii	cc iii
cxxii	xxxvii	cclxxii	ccliii	cl	cclvii
cxcvii	xxxviii	cclviii	cclviiii	clii	ccxlviii
cccc	xxxvii	lxxvii	cclxviii	clii	cliiii
cccci	xxxvii	lxxvii	ccxcviiii	cliiii	ccxcviii
cxxcvii	xxxviiii	lxxviiii	cclxvi	xlii	cccc
cxxcviiii	xliii	clxviii	cclxviii	clx	cclxii
cx liiii	liiii	xc	cclxxvi	clxcii	cclxviii
cxxvii	liiii	xcii	cclxxxvi	clxcii	cclxvi
cxliiii	lvii	xliiii	cclxxxvi	clxcii	cclxvii
cxliii	lvii	xxcvi	cclxxiii	clxcviii	cclxvi
cliiii	lviiii	xxcvii	cclxxcii	clxcviii	clxxviii
cxviiii	iiii	cxliiii	ccci	clxcii	cclxxviii
cxviiii	xcii	xcii	cccviiii	clxcviii	ccci
cxxviiii	lxxvii	ccvii	cccxii	cxcii	cccii
clxc	lxxvii	xcvi	cccxii	cxcvii	cccciii
cxxvii	lxxvii	xclxv	cccviii	cxcvii	cccxcii

21v *(p34)* and the Lion on 191v *(p62)*, the knots open out to allow the insertion of triangular fillers between the circles, a device that is distinctive to Durrow and may reflect the Greek abbreviation for *Deus*, used in 193r *(p65)*.

Ernst Kitzinger has drawn attention to the function of interlace patterns in other cultures. In entrapping evil forces, interlaced knots served a protective or apotropaic function, the addition of an animal head providing enhanced powers. Interlace is used at the entrances to buildings, where protection was particularly needed.[32] The interlaced borders of the Durrow carpet pages at the openings to the Gospels were thus intended, according to this argument, to protect the sacred texts and their authors. In the Book of Durrow, the symbols can be seen as protected by fields of interlaced borders as they stand isolated on grounds of blank vellum.

Carpet pages, present in several of the insular Gospel books, seem to have evolved from the use of blind designs on book covers, such as the binding of a sixth-century Coptic manuscript from a site near Sakkara in Egypt (now Dublin, Chester Beatty Library, MS 815), which resembles Durrow in its use of cross and interlace decoration. In Durrow, folio 248r *(p79)* is most reminiscent of a book cover. A seventh-century (?) manuscript of Orosius from the Irish foundation at Bobbio in northern Italy (now Milan, Biblioteca Ambrosiana, MS D. 23. sup.) contains a page of purely abstract decoration as a frontispiece to the text,[33] indicating the use of such pages in an Irish context at an early date. The cross in varying forms is a recurring motif in Durrow, appearing centrally in the carpet pages 85v *(p48)*, 192v *(p64)* and 248r *(p79)*, and in several less prominent places like the bow of the *M* of *Marcus* on 17r *(p31)*, where it resembles examples in the Cathach or the Book of Kells.

OPPOSITE:
Book of Durrow
folio 8v

COLOPHON PAGE

(folio 247v)

THE COLOPHON OR INSCRIPTION PAGE of the Book of Durrow *(p78)* has attracted considerable attention. The lower colophon in the second column, by the scribe of the manuscript, reads *Ora pro me frater mi dñs tecum sit* ('Pray for me, my brother, the Lord be with you). A further inscription was also the work of the scribe, but was subjected to over-writing, erasure and alterations by more than one hand at an early date, and is no longer susceptible to precise transcription. In A A Luce's transcription and translation it reads:

Rogo beatudinem

tuam sce praesbiter

patrici ut quicumque

hunc libellum manu te

nuerit

meminerit colum

bae scriptoris. qui hoc scripsi

mmet euangelium. per xii

dierum spatium gtia dni nri ss

OPPOSITE:
Book of Durrow
folio 9r

[I ask your beatitude, holy presbyter Patrick, that whoever holds in his hand this little book may remember {me} Columba the writer who wrote this Gospel for myself in the space of 12 days by the grace of our Lord. s.s.]

cccxxii	ccii	cccuiiii	xiiii	iiii	xuii
cccxxxiiii	cccuiiii	cccxuii	ccuii	xxii	ueii
cccxxuiiii	ccxiiii	cccxuii	beui	xuii	ueu
cccxl	ccxx	cccxuiii	el	lxuii	u
cccxlii	ccxxii	cccxxuiii	ebei	lxuiii	xxui
cccxliiii	ccxxiiii	cccxuiii	eber	lxxuii	liii
ccxlii	ccxx ii	cccxx	cc iiii	cxii	xxi
ccliii	ccxxii	cccxxxiii	cc iiii	cxxi	cxxuii
ccliiii	ccxxx iii	cccxxxuii	ccxuii	lxxui	el
			ccxii	cxui	cxxuii

	ccxuii	cxxui	cxxuii
	cccxii	cxxui	cxxuiii
	ccbxxii	cluiii	xxuiii
	ccbxxiii	ebei	lxxii
	ccbxuiii	ebei	xxui
	cexuii	cluiii	cluii
	cexxii	cxluii	cluii
	ccuiii	cxxuiii	lxi
	cccxxiii	cbxx	ciii
	cccuii	cbxxuii	cxxuiii
	cccxxi	cci	cuii
	ccc xei	cci	cuiii
	ccc xeii	ccii	cxxuii
	cccxxxiiii	ccuii	cbxxui
	ccxxiiii	ccuii	cbxxuii
	cccxxeiii	ccxii	cc iii

i	xiiii	i
i	xiiii	iii
i	xiiii	ii
iiii	iiii	ii
iiii	iii	xxii
iiuiiii	icii	ieui
beiiii	icui	xxuiii
xe	iiuii	cxuii
xe	iuii	cccxiiii
xeii	cexl	cii
cei	ccuiii	cxluii
cei	ccuiii	xx
ceii	ceu iiii	eeuii
ceii	ceu iiii	beeuii
ceii	ceu iiii	xeiii
cei	cxu iiii	uei
cei	cxu iiii	uiiii
cei	cxu iiii	beeui
cei	cxu iiii	xx
cxuii	cxu iiii	cbxui
ceii	cxu iiii	ceiii
cxluii	cxii	xiuii

Luce interpreted the final 's.s.' of the inscription as 'subscriptus', meaning 'undersigned'. He suggested that Colum Cille had signed the colophon from which this was copied, and had written 'mei' at the end of line 6. This was probably carried over to the Durrow colophon, but changed later to 'Columbae'. No space was available to make large-scale changes, since a red scrolled line, of the kind familiar from other pages, was at the end of the inscription. This scrolling is barely visible in reproduction.

Clearly the colophon is not a contemporary record of St Colum Cille, and some uncertainty must hover over the evidential value of and intention behind the erased and rewritten lines. Yet it may readily be supposed that a Gospel book written by the founder would be available for copying in a Columban house, especially as Colum Cille had a reputation as a skilful and prolific scribe, and even a copy made from such a book would be regarded as an important relic to enhance the status of the monastery. The reference to '12 days' may be taken as an indication that the exemplar was of one Gospel only, or as an exaggeration of the scribe's speed. [34]

Cathach, folio 50v *(Royal Irish Academy, MS 12.R.33)*

OPPOSITE:
Book of Durrow
folio 15r

carne nascentis per universa
legentes intellegant atque id ineo
itaquo adprehensi sunt et adprae
hendere expetunt recognoscant no
bis enim hoc instat do argumentum sunt
et fidem faciat et ne ad eo pe
ranur di intellegendam esse diligent
dispossitionem quae tenetub: non tace

ERAT Iohannis bapti
zatis in aduentus super
eum sps di et futurus
in deserto temptatus
Apostquam traditus est Iohannis
praedicauit et uocauit disci
pulos et hominem absp inmun
do curauit
... et ... ub erant
et quaerebant eum turbae
ut saluarentur ... eum
Rogauit ih inla eprosus et mundauit
et sanans pancta cum dpexter tol
egnabatur inuum et uade

239

Summary

of

Decorated

Pages

THE MANUSCRIPT OPENS with an image of a double-armed cross embedded in a field of interlace and bordered by panels of interlace, folio 1v *(p10)*. This faces folio 2r *(p15)*, again containing a cross, around which the four Evangelist symbols are disposed. A page of abstract decoration, usually known as a 'carpet' page, of trumpet and spiral forms, is at folio 3v *(p18)*. On folios 8r to 10r *(p27)* are canon tables, which follow a scheme drawn up by Eusebius (*c* 260–*c* 340) while bishop of Caesarea from *c* 315. Eusebius divided the Gospels into sections, each roughly equivalent to three verses of the system in current use. Matthew had 355 sections, Mark had 233, Luke had 342 and John had 232. The canon tables provided a harmony whereby a passage or incident occurring in one Gospel could, in theory, be located in another. In Durrow, the canons are laid out in a grid formation, similar to folios 5v and 6r of the Book of Kells *(p36)*. The numbers in the Durrow canon tables, or a 'clone' of them, acted as the model for the numbers in the Book of Kells.[35]

 The Gospels, with many corrections in a contemporary hand, are in a version which is close to the Vulgate text compiled late in the fourth

& cum dixisset petro ueni me se qua
bis ad onore neue ii cus iitem
ptationem

Cum ducentur iñs ad caïfan qui
dam saeque batur ad fecatis sin
donem & ductus est iñs ad passione

Post resurrectionem apparuit
apostolis & dixit qui crediderit
& baptizatus fuerit saluus erit
qui non crediderit dam nabitur &
receptus in caelis dñs ---

[faint erased lines]

MARCUS euangelista
dī & petri in bab
tismate filiusq: in divi
no sermone discipulus sacerdotium
in israhel agens secundum carnem
leuita ad versus ad fidem xpi euan
gelium in italia scribsit ostendens
in eo quid & generi suo deberet &
xpo hammi nauum principium uoce
prophetice exclamationis instru
ens ordinem leuiticae electionis

can putasse· sibiposthdem pri
cem dicitur utsacerdotio nep nob·
habentur sectantum consenuent
fidei praedistinata pouintelectio
ut necsic inopenetenbi pendidens
quod priusmenuenat ingenere
nam alexandriae episcopus fuit
cuius pensingula opisscine &eu
angeli insedicta disponene &dis
ciplinam inselegis cognosceneest
& diuinam dni incanne intellegene
natumam quae&nos primum ne
quint dehincinquista uolumus
agnosci habentes menaclem exchor
tationis quoniam quiplantat &
quirrurigat unum sunt quiautem
inchementum praestatasest ⁓

Incipit argumentum euangeli
secundum lucam · ⌇⌇⌇⌇⌇⌇

LUCAS SYRUS ⌇⌇⌇⌇⌇⌇⌇
natione ante ochensis
arte medicus discipu
lus apostolorum postea
paulum saecutus usq: adconfes
onem eius seruiens do sinecrimine
mamueq: uxonem num quam·

242

...imostacem; quoniam uolenti

bur c[on]demonstrano uidetur

quamras adclienab; pnodidisse

HiCest iohannis euangelir

 taunis electrodecim

discipulis di quiuirgo electur

adeo est quemdenubas nubene

uolentem Reuocauitdeus cuius uirgini

tatis inhoc duplex testimonium in

euangelio datur quod &prae ceteris

dilectus adeo dicitur &huic matrem

suam iens adcrucem commendauit

d[omi]ns utuirginem uirgo seruaret · De

niq; manifestans ineuangelio quod

erat ipse incorruptibilis uerbi opus

inchoans solus uerbum caro fac

tum esse nec lucem atenebris fuisse

conprehensam testatur primum

signum ponens quod innubtis fe

cit d[omin]us utostendens quod erat ipse

lectoribus demonstraret quod ubi ·

d[omin]us inuitatur deficerenubtarum

uinum debeatur enib; inmutaus

century by St Jerome at the request of Pope Damasus. While the text appears to be distinct from versions contained in other insular Gospel books, much essential comparative work remains to be done in this area. The Gospels are prefaced by a page depicting the symbol of each Evangelist, followed by a carpet page (except for Matthew), and, facing it, the decorated opening words of the text.

St Matthew's Gospel is heralded by his symbol, the Man, on folio 21v *(p34)*, facing the opening words of his Gospel, *LIBER GENERA / tionis* ('The book of the generation [of Jesus Christ]': Mt 1.1) on folio 22r *(p37)*. The words *CHRISTI AUTEM generatio sic erat* ('Now the generation of Christ was in this wise': Mt 1.18) are given emphasis at the opening to St Matthew's account of the birth of Christ on folio 23r *(p39)*.

The Eagle on folio 84v *(p42)*, acting as St Mark's symbol, is followed by a carpet page of interlaced circles, folio 85v *(p48)*, which faces an elaboration of the opening words of his Gospel, *INITIUM / EUANGE/LII IHU XPI* ('The beginning of the Gospel of Jesus Christ': Mk 1.1) on 86r *(p49)*.

St Luke's symbol, the Calf, is on folio 124v *(p56)*. A carpet page of

Bronze and enamel mount from the Oseberg tomb wooden bucket *(University Museum of National Antiquities, Oslo, Norway)*

LEFT:
Book of Durrow
folio 21v (detail)
OPPOSITE:
Book of Durrow
folio 21v

interlace with inlaid rectangular panels is on 125v *(p58)*, facing the opening of St Luke's Gospel on folio 126r *(p59)*, *QUONIAM / QUIDEM MUL / ti* ('Forasmuch as many have taken in hand to set forth in order a narration of the things that have been accomplished among us': Lk 1.1). The following words are also emphasised on folio 23r *(p39)*: *FUIT IN DIEBUS / HERODIS REGIS / iudae* ('There was in the days of Herod the king of Judea': Lk 1.5).

St John's Gospel is prefaced by his symbol, the Lion, on folio 191v *(p62)*. The carpet page associated with this Gospel, folio 192v *(p64)*, is perhaps the most striking, and certainly the most frequently reproduced, single page in the Book of Durrow. It faces the opening words of St John's Gospel, *IN PRIN/CIPIO / ERAT UERBUM ET UER/BUM ERAT AP / UD DEUM ET DEUS* ('In the beginning was the Word, and the Word was with God, and the Word was God': Jn 1.1).

A further carpet page, folio 248r *(p79)*, composed of 'lattice' work with crosses, is at the end of the manuscript, though it may not have been there originally. This is a most unorthodox position, at least insofar as can be

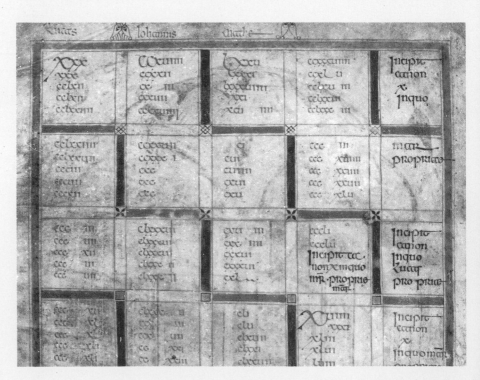

Book of Kells, folio 5v: canon tables *(Trinity College Library, Dublin)*

OPPOSITE:
Book of Durrow
folio 22r

LIBERGENERA
tionis ihuxpi filii
dauid filii abraham;
abraham genuit isa
ac isaac autem genuit iacob ia
cob autem genuit iudam et frat
res eius iudas autem genuit pha
res et zaram de thamar phares
autem genuit esrom esrom aute
genuit aram aram autem genuit
aminadab aminadab autem
genuit naasson autem genuit
salmon salmon autem genuit
booz de rachab booz autem ge
nuit obed ex ruth obed autem ge
nuit iesse iesse autem genuit
dauid regem dauid autem rex
genuit salomonem ex ea quae
fuit uriae salomon autem genuit

14

judged from surviving examples of insular Gospel books, and it may represent later work.

Some uncertainty attaches to the present position of other leaves. As with the Book of Kells, several of Durrow's major pages were executed on single leaves. These could easily become detached and misplaced. Damage to the spine folds caused by the shrine, and subsequent trimming to facilitate binding when the shrine disappeared, left the manuscript as a collection of single leaves. Some pages were clearly placed in the wrong position. The symbol of the Man, for example, now folio 21v, formed the last leaf of the book, while the present last leaf, folio 248, was folio 13. As a result, there is disagreement regarding the correct location of certain pages. In particular, while it is agreed that St Matthew's Gospel must originally have had a carpet page, it is not clear whether this is lost or whether it was the present 1v or 248r (though this formed a bifolium with folio 247) or, as seems more likely, folio 3v.[36]

In the prefatory material, certain initials are enlarged for decorative effect. On folio 4r *(p21)*, the words *NOUUM OPUS* are displayed in a band at the opening of St Jerome's letter to Pope Damasus concerning his Gospel text. On 6v, the abbreviated set of glossaries, or interpretations of Hebrew names[37] in Matthew, beginning with the letter *b*, are emboldened and decorated with spirals, while the first word of the text, *Bartholomeus*, is emphasised with red dotting and diminuendo. The same dotting, trumpet and spiral and diminuendo techniques are used on *Natiuitas*, the opening word of the *Breues causae* (accumulations of section headings) of Matthew on 11r; on *Mattheus*, the opening word of the *Argumentum* (text characterising the Evangelists) of Matthew on 14r;[38] on *Et erat* at the opening of the *Breues causae* of Mark on 15r *(p29)*; on *Marcus*, the opening word of the *Argumentum* of Mark on 17r *(p31)*; on the opening of the *Argumentum* of Luke on folio 18r *(p32)*, *Lucas syrus*, where the words are contained within dotted lines; on *Hic est*, the beginning of the *Argumentum* of John on 19v *(p33)*; on *Enom* in the Hebrew names for John and Mark on 20v; on *Uespere* (Mt 28.1) on 82v; and on *Zachariae* (*Breues causae* of Luke) on 242v. The decoration of *Iohannis* (*Breues causae* of John) on 246r *(p75)* has been damaged by abrasion.

OPPOSITE:
Book of Durrow
folio 23r

nuit iacob iacob autem genuit io
seph uirum mariae de qua na
tus est ihs qui uocatur xps

Omnes ergo generationes ab ra
cham usque ad dauid generationes
xiiii et a dauid usque ad trans mig
rationem babilonis generation
es xiiii et a trans migratione babi
lonis usque ad xpm generationes xiiii

Xpi autem

generatio sic erat
cum esset et disp on
sata mater eius maria se
ph ante quam conuenirent in
uentaest in utero habens de spu
sco

Ioseph autem uir eius cum esse
iustus et nollet eam traducere
uoluit occulte dimittere eam

bibeus sedeneautem addexteno
meam autadsinistram nonesteu
dareuobis sedquib: paratum est
apatrem eo ~ ~~~~~~~~~~~~~~~

Audientes illidicem indignatisu
ntdeduob: fratrib: ihsautemuoca
uiteos adse Scitis eius quiaprin
cipesgentium dominantur eonum
& quimaiores sunt potestatem
exercent ineos nonitaeritinteruos
sedquicumqueuoluerit interuos
maionfieri situestrer minister &
quiuoluerit interuos primusesse
erituesterseruus sicutfilius homi
nis nonuenit ministrari sedminis
trare & dareanimam suam rede
ptionem pronomultis ~ ~~~~~~~~

Egredientib: eisabiericho seq
aut est eum turba multa Ecce
duocaecisedentes saecus inuiamau
dierunt quiaihs transinet & cla
mauerunt dicentes dne misere
renostri filidauid turbaautem
increpabateos uttacerent at
illimagis clamabant dicentesdne

Rubrics (introductions and conclusions delineated in red) mark the beginning and end of texts on folios 4r *(p21)*, 6v, 7v, 9r/v *(p27)*, 10r, 11r, 14r, 15r *(p29)*, 17r *(p31)*, 18r *(p32)*, 19v *(p33)*, 22r *(p37)*, 84r, 86r *(p49)*, 123v, 126r *(p59)* and 191r *(p61)*.[39] Other minor decorative techniques are employed throughout the text. The opening word of a section is slightly enlarged and denoted by red dotting and diminuendo. Spirals are used as terminals to some initial letters. Red scrolling flourishes of varying length, very similar to those in the Echternach Gospels *(below)*, are employed throughout the manuscript as line-fillers. On 124r *(p55)*, the first entry in the glossary of Hebrew names in Luke, *Agusti sollemniter stantes*, is enlarged as though to act as a heading. This page, written, as Lowe judged it, in a less formal script than the rest of the book, is also divided with red vertical, zig-zag lines (in one place a dotted line), which may have functioned as text dividers in Durrow's exemplar, but act as decorative devices in this context. On 134v such lines do serve to divide one text from another, while horizontal dotted lines lead the eye across the page.

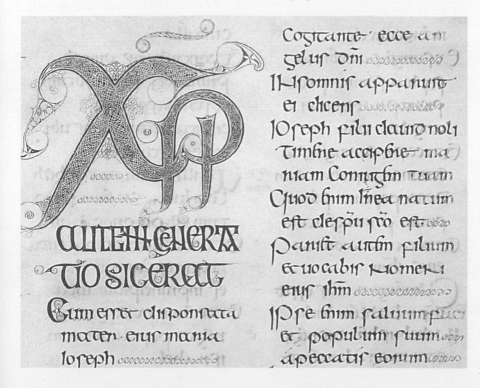

Echternach Gospels, folio 19r: Chi-Rho *(Bibliothèque Nationale, Paris, lat. 9389)*

OPPOSITE:
Book of Durrow
folio 61v

Symbols
of the
Evangelists

THE ORIGIN OF DURROW'S Evangelist symbols lies in two biblical texts. From the Old Testament, the prophecy of Ezekiel read:

> . . . behold, a whirlwind came out of the north, and a great cloud, and a fire . . . and in the midst thereof the likeness of four living creatures . . . there was the face of a man, and the face of a lion on the right side of all the four; and the face of an ox, on the left side of all the four; and the face of an eagle over all the four . . . and their wings were stretched upward, two wings of every one were joined, and two covered their bodies . . . And above the firmament . . . was the likeness of a throne . . . and upon the likeness of the throne, was the likeness as of the appearance of a man above upon it. (Ezekiel 1.4–26 *passim*)

Encouraged by the explanation of Ezekiel 2.1 that 'This was the vision of the likeness of the glory of the Lord', commentators came to understand the vision as that of Christ in glory adored by the four beings.

From the New Testament, the Apocalypse of St John described a vision in which similar creatures appeared:

> . . . and in the sight of the throne was as it were a sea of glass like to crystal, and in the midst of the throne and round about the throne were four living creatures full of eyes before and behind. And the first living creature was like a

Pair of Gothic gold enamel saddle attachments dating from the fifth century *(Museum of National History, Bucharest, Romania)*

OPPOSITE:
Book of Durrow
folio 84v

lion: and the second living creature like a calf: and the third living creature, having the face, as it were, of a man: and the fourth living creature was like an eagle flying. And the four living creatures had each of them six wings: and round about and within they are full of eyes. And they rested not day and night, saying: 'Holy, Holy, Holy, Lord God Almighty, who was, and who is, and who is to come.' (Apocalypse 4. 6–8)

The creatures of the prophecies became identified with the Evangelists as early as the second century through the writings of St Irenaeus, bishop of Lyons (c 130–200). Irenaeus compared the creatures to the four regions of the cosmos and the four winds, which together symbolised the spread of the Gospels.[40]

St Gregory's fourth-century commentary on Ezekiel identified the symbols as the four stages in Christ's life. Christ was a man in being born, a calf in the manner of his death, a lion in the power of his resurrection, and an eagle in ascending to Heaven. In his prefaces to the Gospels, St Jerome identified them in the way which became familiar to those who decorated and read Gospel manuscripts: the Man symbolised St Matthew, the Lion symbolised St Mark, the Calf St Luke and the Eagle St John. In a reversion to the pre-Vulgate order of Irenaeus's scheme, St John's Gospel in the Book of Durrow is introduced by the Lion, and St Mark's by the Eagle. In folio 2r (p15), where the four symbols are arranged around an interlaced cross, the pre-Vulgate order applies so long as the symbols are read anti-clockwise. If, on the other hand, the symbols are read clockwise, they are placed in the Vulgate order. It is not impossible that the ambiguity was intentional.

DOUBLE-ARMED CROSS

(folio 1v)

EVANGELIST SYMBOLS AROUND CROSS

(folio 2r)

DURROW IS IN THE TRADITION of Coptic manuscripts in prefacing the Gospels with a cross. On 1v *(p10)* a double-armed cross, without a supporting base, is framed by and imposed on a field of interlace. The central boxes of its eight squares are filled with decoration, the six external boxes with checkered patterns, the two internal boxes with step patterns. Repeated cross forms act as a secondary focus. Four stepped crosses filled with interlace are placed in the corners of the frame.

On an iconographical level, the cross functioned as a reminder of Christ's crucifixion and death, the eight squares of 1v perhaps recalling the eighth day of the Passion, the day of Resurrection. Martin Werner suggested further that Durrow 1v was intended to act as 'a highly abstract representation of the fragments and titulus of the True Cross displayed on the altar of the church of Golgotha in the Holy Sepulchre complex for the solemn Good Friday *Adoratio Crucis* ceremony'.[41] The image corresponds to the eye-witness account of the Holy Places by the Gaulish bishop Arculf, who was shipwrecked on Iona, and whose account formed the basis of the *De locis sanctis* of Adomnán, ninth abbot of Iona and biographer of Colum Cille. Adomnán was preparing his text between 682 and 686, a period that Werner judged to be consistent with the production of the book. Relics of the True Cross were commonly housed in the Middle Ages in shrines shaped like double-armed crosses, examples of which survive from Ireland.[42]

The decoration of 1v has several parallels. The image resembles one in a sixteenth-century illustrated Persian Diatessaron, or Gospel harmony (Florence, Bibl. Laur. Or. MS 81, folio 127), which is presumed to have been inspired by earlier models. In theme, though not in style, 1v resembles the eight-circle cross page of the Book of Kells folio 33r. Many comparisons were provided by Werner, such as the Merovingian double-barred cross from the reliquary of Ste-Croix at Poitiers.[43] The stylistic model for 1v may have been a double-armed version of the enamelled Antrim Cross in the Hunt Museum, Limerick *(p46)*.[44] In a matter of detail, the interlocking T-bars of a recently discovered enamel mount, probably eighth-century, from Lough Derravaragh, County Westmeath *(p11)*, (National Museum of Ireland, E 499: 325), are close to the two central squares of Durrow 1v.

Folio 2r *(p15)* carries a complex image of the Evangelist symbols arrayed around a cross, with enlarged terminals in a frame of patterned lozenges. It should be read in conjunction with folio 1v facing it. Folio 2r has a distinctive ornamented base which represents, Werner suggested, the marble steps on the Golgotha hill leading pilgrims to the great cross studded with jewels (the *crux gemmata*), which was erected in the year 421 on the orders of the emperor Theodosius. The form and colouring given the cross in

Antrim Cross
(Hunt Museum, Limerick)

2r resemble the stepped *crux gemmata* in a Syriac manuscript dated 1177, where the cross is placed in a border of interlace, with the names of the Evangelists around it *(p47)*, (Dublin, Chester Beatty Library: Syriac, MS 703, folio 11r).

In various biblical interpretations, the symbols of the Evangelists were identified with the four rivers of Paradise, where the tree of life (the Crucifixion cross) grew.[45] The symbols of 2r, not drawn with great delicacy, were described by Westwood in 1843 as 'probably the rudest and most grotesque delineations of the sacred symbols ever executed'.[46] They resemble only partially those found prefacing their Gospels. The Eagle, the only symbol given a halo, most strongly resembles the composition on 84v *(p42)*. The Man resembles 21v *(p34)* in his hairstyle and checkered cloak, but his right hand is visible, folded across his chest.[47] The Calf's body is patterned in a manner similar to the Man, but his frontal depiction, horns and triangular composition are entirely at variance with the naturalistic style of the animal on 124v *(p56)*, though they do resemble the Calf in the central arch of the

Syriac Gospel book, MS 703, folio 11r *(Chester Beatty Library, Dublin)*

LEFT:
Book of Durrow
folio 85v (detail)
FOLLOWING PAGES:
Book of Durrow
folios 85v, 86r

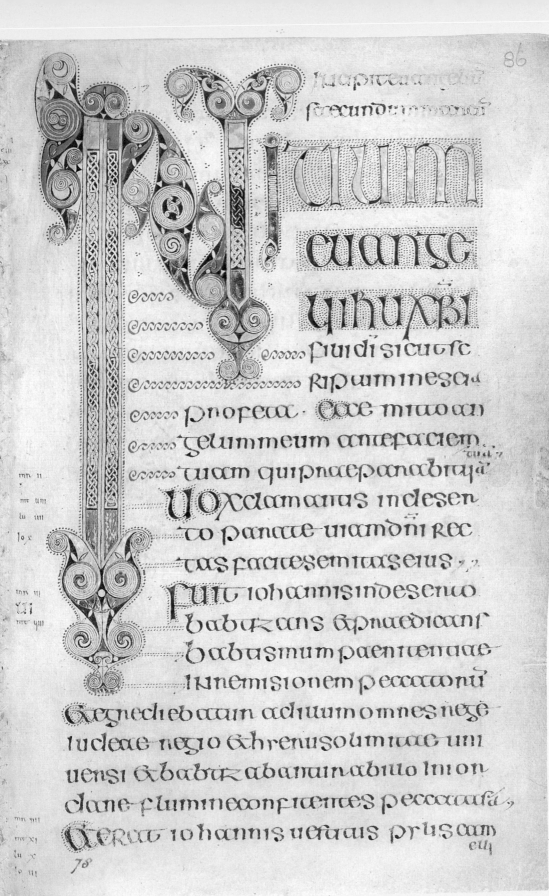

INitium
euange
lii ihu xpi
filii di sicut sc
riptum in esa
propheta · ecce mitto an
gelum meum ante faciem
tuam qui praeparabit uia
Uox clamantis in desen
to parate uiam dni rec
tas facite semitas eius
Fuit iohannis in deserto
babtizans & praedicans
babtismum paenitentiae
in remisionem peccatorum
Egrediebatur ad illum omnes rege
iudeae regio & hierusolimitae uni
uensi & babtizabantur ab illo in ion
dane flumine confitentes peccata sua
& erat iohannis uestitus pilis cam
eli

Book of Kells folio 4r. The Lion is also given a frontal pose, but resembles the creature of 191v *(p62)* in having his fur represented by lozenges, a feature that can occasionally be seen on costumes in the Book of Kells, for example in that of the small man seated on a stone on 8r. The 2r symbols resemble to some extent those of the eighth-century Lichfield Gospels, p219, or the Soiscél Molaise shrine, where the symbols, as on 2r, have an upright frontal pose.

Book of Durrow
folio 86r (detail)

Belt-buckle from Lagore
crannog, County Meath
*(National Museum of Ireland,
E14: 213)*

CARPET PAGE

with

TRUMPET

SPIRALS

(folio 3v)

PERHAPS MISPLACED from opposite the opening to St Mathew's Gospel, folio 3v *(p18)* is dominated by two large trumpet and spiral devices at the centre of the page, with smaller pairs of similar devices above and below. All six discs are held together by long, elegant trumpets with floral terminals. The border is composed of complex six-ribbon interlace, with four knots within each roundel. The top border and background of the page have been lost, perhaps damaged while the manuscript was enclosed in its shrine. The discs resemble the escutcheons of bronze hanging bowls, the heads of insular hand-pins, and the spirals of the Lagore belt-buckle *(p50)*.[48] A particularly close parallel is a bronze bowl from the eighth century found at Jaatten in Norway but perhaps originating in Ireland.[49] A total of forty-two spirals appears on the page. Henderson has linked this number, and the forty-two animals on folio 192v *(p64)*, with the forty-two generations of Christ enumerated in St Matthew's Gospel, 1.1–17.[50]

DECORATED PAGES

of

ST MATTHEW'S GOSPEL

(folios 21v, 22r, 23r)

THE HEAD AND GARMENT of the Man on 21v *(p34)* are placed in a frontal pose, though the position of his feet suggests that he is moving to his right, in a manner similar to the figure on the Ballyvourney slab in County Cork or figures on the Papil stone at Burra in Shetland.[51] His face is shaded through the skilful use of dotting patterns. His arms and neck are not visible due to the shape given his cloak, which resembles an Irish ecclesiastical bell. His beard and hair are indicated with fine lines. It is not clear whether he has a tonsure or simply a centre parting. The Irish tonsure, rejected for the north of England at the Synod of Whitby in 664, persisted in Irish ecclesiastical circles into the eighth century. It seems to have involved shaving the front of the head, with the hair allowed to grow long at the back, while the Roman tonsure took the form of a crown. The man is shod in low boots with a high back, a simpler version of the boots worn by St Matthew in an eighth-century Irish manuscript now in St Gall, Switzerland (Stiftsbibliothek, MS 1395, p418). His cloak and leggings are decorated with lines of bold checkers, those on the cloak interspersed with panels of less dense pen and ink ornament composed of squares, crosses, lozenges and (in the lowest panel) circles. These patterns mimic the technique of millefiori glass rods, and bear resemblance to metal objects such as a bronze and enamel mount *(p35)* from the Oseberg tomb wooden bucket, now in the University Museum of National Antiquities, Oslo.

The border is filled with broad, rolling ribbon interlace which recalls, as do the man's head and garment, the east face of the Carndonagh cross,[52] though Durrow adds its characteristic triangles as fillers. The external frame around the border differs from those of the other symbols, including 2r *(p15)* and 248r *(p79)*, in not being tapered at the corners.

The opening words of St Matthew's Gospel, *LIBER GENERA / tionis* ('The book of the generation [of Jesus Christ]': Mt 1 1) on folio 22r *(p37)* are the least ambitious of the initial pages, in that only one line of text is

Book of Durrow
folio 121r (detail)

elaborated. Their treatment is comparable in scale and technique to the beginning of Matthew's account of the nativity on 23r *(p39)*, where the Greek monogram of the name of Christ (Chi and Rho) is emphasised at its first appearance. The Chi is further distinguished with a cross. The initial letters on each page are ringed with red dots, with triangles of dots in the background. Red stippling is placed between and within the bands of letters, with the exception of the *B* of *LIBER* on 22r, which is left blank, and the *A* of *AUTEM* on 23r, which encloses a triquetra knot, a symbol of the Trinity.

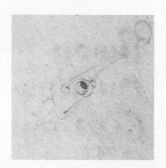

Book of Durrow
folio 124v (detail)

Ricemarch Psalter
folio 2v (detail)
(Trinity College Dublin, MS 50)

OPPOSITE:
Book of Durrow
folio 124r

aaron	mons fortium
anna	gratia eius
asser	beatus
amos	onerans
acheldema	nobiscus · · tione
angelus	sanans de populo
caelum	homo vincens
camuus	populus abiectus
caesar	possessio principalis
caenenez	henecles
cosam	cliuinans
cinam	luctus
capharnau	agen consulationis
chebri	transitus
henochis	pellicus
elisabeth	di mei saturitas
heli gr	ascendens
elmadadi	di mensura uigilans
enam	oculus eonum
helistae	di salus
fanuel	facies dī cha
fase	transitus syd nos diam par
filippus	or lampadis
gabriel	fortitudo dī siue confortati godi
galilaea	galilaea uoluabilis
gennesar	salus bona num
iuineae	montandae
ionelanis	discensus
iony	columba mea
iotanum	dns exultans
iohanna	dns gratia eius
ianuus	illuminans onis
lisanue	nocturnas tempstati
lamec	humilis
lazarus	adiutus
matthata	domum dī
melchi	rex meus
mathusala	mortuus est emisit
malachiel	laudans dnm bnu
manhena	prouocans dmpule
niniui	incas spriosi tae
petrus	agnoscens
pontius	declinans consilium
pilatus	os malleatoris
ros	caput

pam	sublimis
richa	ebrietas
salman	pax
sulon	misit
siuepta	
sem	nomen
sunepta	incensa siue angustia
	panis
simon	pon an chronon
sussanna	lylum
sumantue	custodes
satan	aduersarius siue transgres son
suba	capitur
sadducaei	iustificati

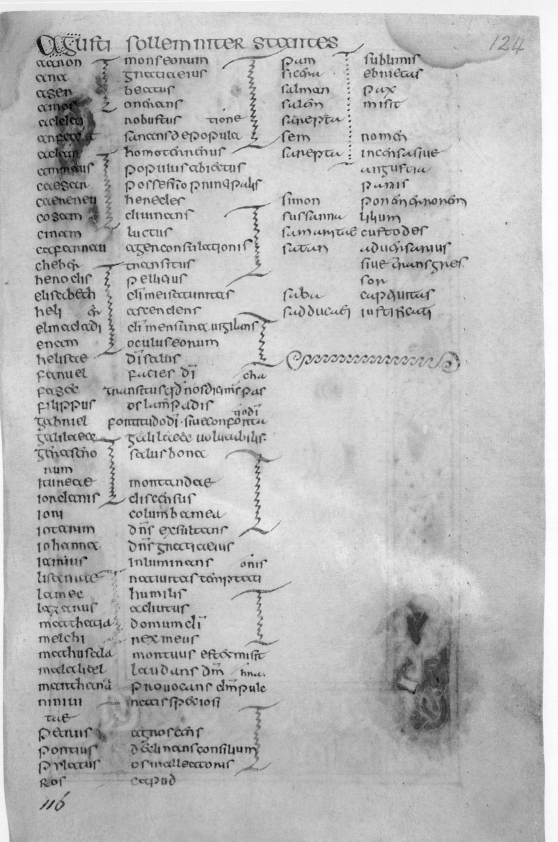

Conall ꝺaᵹeocᵹaɪn �7 ꝺabᴅ gᴅ ɪon
beaᴅᴅaᴅ 7 mɪnmaᴅ ꝼᴅ neᴅlac mᵹᴅ 1633

DECORATED PAGES

of

ST MARK'S

GOSPEL

(folios 84v, 85v, 86r)

DURROW'S EAGLE on 84v *(p42)* is highly stylised, with a round head and eye. An ear is indicated within the circle of the head. His head and feet turn to the right, though his body is depicted frontally. The wings have a cellular structure close to that of garnet *cloisonné* work. The wing tips are indicated with fine lines. In manuscript art he resembles the Eagle in the eighth-century Book of Dimma (Trinity College Dublin, MS 59, p104), but the closest parallels are to be found in late Roman and in many examples of Germanic jewellery. There is a resemblance to a pair of Gothic gold enamel saddle attachments dating from the fifth century in the Museum of National History, Bucharest, Romania *(p43)*.[53]

The carpet page on 85v *(p48)* has fifteen circles composed of and filled with interlace strands, linked with angular interlace which comes

OPPOSITE:
Book of Durrow
folio 124v
FOLLOWING PAGES:
Book of Durrow
folios 125v, 126r

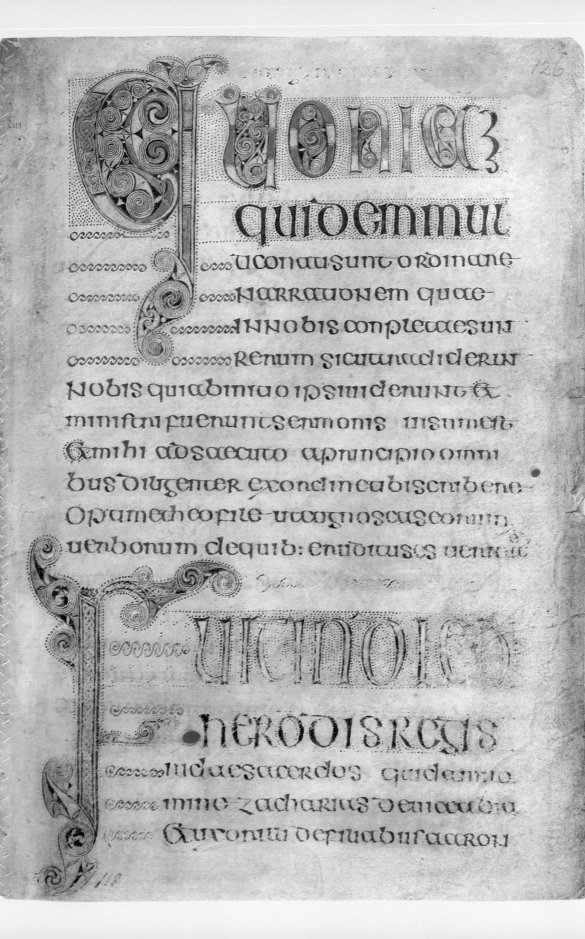

Quoniam
quidem mul
ti conati sunt ordinare
narrationem quae
in nobis conpletae sun
rerum sicut tradiderun
nobis qui ab initio ipsi uiderunt et
ministri fuerunt sermonis uisum est
et mihi adsecuto a principio omni
bus diligenter ex ordine tibi scribe
optime theofile ut cognoscas eorum
uerborum de quib; eruditus es uerita

Fuit in die
bus herodis regis
iudae sacerdos quidam no
mine zacharias de uice abia
et uxor illi de filiabus aaron

together in lozenges. Fourteen of the circles enclose sets of four knots, while the central circle encloses a cross with interlaced terminals on a background of step patterns. Yellow 'rivets' in the centre of the circle can be read as a further cross. There is a strong resemblance in the interlace, as Henry observed, to the oldest surviving part of the Domhnach Airgid reliquary and to the west side of the Fahan Mura slab.[54] There is a slender border of interlace, with alternating stretches dotted, and extensions at the corners of the frame.

The opening words of Mark are elaborated to a greater extent than Matthew, with the first shaft of the *IN* of *INITIUM* stretching three-quarters of the page. Three lines of text are placed on a background of dots, in contrast to the single lines of 22r *(p37)* and 23r *(p39)*. The second *I* is smaller than the *IN*, conforming to the principle of diminuendo, though the gradation is sharp. The terminals of the *IN* and the cross-bar of the *N* are filled with trumpet and spiral decoration. The spirals, in particular at the centre of the cross-bar, resemble bosses found in such metalwork as the St Germain plaque.[55] There is a concentration on red and yellow. Green is used only once, at the top of the *IN* ligature.

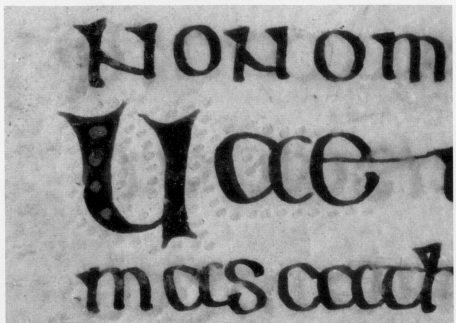

Book of Durrow
folio 158r (detail)
OPPOSITE:
Book of Durrow
folio 191r

uos autem sedete in ciuitate quoad
usque induamini uirtute exalto
Eduxit autem eos foras in bethani
am & eleuatis manib; suis benedixit
eis & factum est dum benediceret
illis recessit ab eis & ferebatur in
caelum & ipsi adorantes regressi
sunt in hierusalem cum gaudio mag
no & erant semper in templo laudan
tes & benedicentes dnm , amen

Explicit euangelium
secundum lucam
Incipit secundum iohannem

+ miserere dne nomini +
173
+ pti necti +

Decorated pages of St Luke's Gospel

(folios 124v, 125v, 126r)

THE CALF on folio 124v *(p56)*, a naturalistic depiction, walks to his right on dainty little feet, red dotting giving him a speckled appearance, which Dr Whitfield has recently likened to animals in filigree work, such as on the Hunterston brooch.[56] There is a strong resemblance to the Calf of the Echternach Gospels folio 115v *(p63)*, though the joints of the two animals differ. Those on Echternach are scrolled, while Durrow's are indicated by interlocking trumpet spirals, to which a remote archetype, or at least a parallel, from the late Roman world may be found in Sassanian silverwork from the third and fourth centuries, exemplified by a charging boar and dogs on a silver strip (British Museum, WΛΛ, 123063) which may have acted as a clothing attachment.[57]

A drawing, almost a 'doodle', lightly executed in ink in the ground

Echternach Gospels, folio 115v: the Calf, symbol of St Luke *(Bibliothèque Nationale, Paris, lat. 9389)*

OPPOSITE:
Book of Durrow
folio 191v
FOLLOWING PAGES:
Book of Durrow
folios 192v, 193r

above the Calf, has not previously been discussed. It bears some resemblance to the Lion head inset on a wing of the Calf in the early ninth-century Book of Armagh folio 68,[58] but its closest parallel is with motifs in the late eleventh-century Ricemarch Psalter *(p54)*, (Trinity College Dublin, MS 50).

The carpet page for Luke, folio 125v *(p58)*, is set in a border of interlace, with jaw-like extensions at each corner. Each border is connected, in a manner that resembles a cross, to broader four-strand interlace in the centre of the page, which settles into the form of eight 'quadrilobes', to use Nordenfalk's phrase.[59] The page is balanced by the inset of eight rectangular panels executed in pen and ink, owing much in inspiration to metalwork, and resembling mounts from the Sutton Hoo sword belt.[60] The two lower vertical panels resemble the chevron millefiori-style checkering of the frame of Durrow 2r *(p15)*, executed more crudely on 248r *(p79)*. The horizontal panels on the left can be read as swastikas or as stepped crosses, while the corresponding insets on the right of the page resemble *cloisonné* glass. Water damage being less severe here than in other areas of the book, the green pigment has largely remained intact, apart from some degradation at the lower right corner.

The opening words of Luke are the most balanced of the Gospel initials in terms of colour. The diminuendo of *Quoniam* is more gradual than that of Mark, while the shaft of the Q stretches through six lines of text. The page is balanced with the decoration of *FUIT IN DIEBUS / HERODIS REGIS* (Lk 1.5), which has been damaged by rubbing. The rubric at the top of the page, *Euangelium saecundum Lucam* ['the Gospel according to Luke'] has become largely illegible.

OPPOSITE:
Book of Durrow
folio 205r

bene enauauerunt foenum multum in
loco discum buerunt ergo uiri numero
quasi quinq̄ milia Accepit ergo pa
nes ihs & cum gratias egisset distribuit
discum bentib: similiter & ex piscib:
quantum uolebant ut autem inple
sunt dixit discipulis suis colligite
quae superuenerunt fragmenta
ne pereant Collegerunt ergo & imple
uerunt duodecim cophinos fraug
mentorum ex quinq̄ panib" ordea
cii quae superauerunt his qui
manducauerunt

Illi ergo homines cum uidissent
quod fecerat signum dicebat quia
hic est uere propheta qui uenturus es
in hunc mundum Ihs ergo cum cog
nouisset quia uenturi essent ut ra
perent eum & facerent eum regem

fugit iterum in montem ipse solus
ut autem sero factum est discendo
runt discipuli eius ad mare & cum
ascendissent nauem uenerunt
trans mare in capharnaum & tenebr
ae iam factae erant & non uen eum &

DECORATED PAGES *of* ST JOHN'S GOSPEL

(folios 191v, 192v, 193r)

THE LION OF MARK on 191v *(p62)* is a formal figure resembling a boar, an animal that would have been familiar to the artist. His fur is composed of alternating red and green lozenges. His joints are like those of Pictish stone carvings, particularly the beast on the cross slab at Papil, Shetland,[61] but, unlike the majority of Pictish animals, Durrow's Lion walks to his right.[62] As Robert Stevenson pointed out, similar animals in manuscript art probably acted as models for the Pictish sculptors.[63] The Lion's outline, joints and the lower end of his tail are in yellow. His tail curls back behind his head. His face and underbelly are dotted (this is reflected in parts of the interlaced border), and red is painted between his toes. His mouth is open, his tongue protruding in a manner common to the insular Lion and indeed much of early Christian imagery. The prominence of the tongue may be an allusion to

OPPOSITE:
Book of Durrow
folio 234r

Calice inquen dedit mihi pater

non biba · illum ·

Cohors ergo & tribunus & ministri

iudaeorum conpraehenderunt

ihin · & alligauerunt eum ·

& adduxerunt eum ad annam pri

mum erat enim socer caifae · qui

erat pontifex anni illius erat autem

caifas qui consilium dederat

iudaeis quia expedit unum homi

nem mori · pro populo ·

Sequebatur autem ihin · petrus

& alius discipulus ·

Discipulus autem ille erat notus

pontifici · & introiuit cum ihin in

atrium pontificis ·

Petrus autem stabat ad ostium foris ·

Exiuit ergo discipulus alius qui

notus pontifici & dixit ostiariae ·

& introduxit petrum ·

Dicit ergo petro ancilla hostia

ria num quid & tu ex discipulis es

hominis istius dicit ille non sum ·

Stabant autem serui & ministri

ad prunas · quia frigus erat · &

254

224

the last words of Christ's ancestor King David, 'The spirit of the Lord hath spoken by me, and his word by my tongue' (2 Kings 23.2), or to several passages in Psalms, such as 'My tongue shall pronounce thy word' (Ps 118.172). In style, the Lion resembles the Lion of the Trier Gospels folio 1v,[64] and has a compelling though most puzzling resemblance to an eighteenth- or nineteenth-century wooden lion clad with silver sheet from the treasure of King Gbehanzin of Dahomey, West Africa.[65]

Ardagh Chalice (detail)
(National Museum of Ireland)

Folio 192v *(p64)* is a composition of extraordinary impact. There are two panels top and tail, and one on either side forming a square. In the square floats a double-bordered medallion filled with ribbon interlace and, at its centre, a static cross to which the eye is drawn irresistibly. A triangle of circular devices like glass studs is placed around the cross, in a manner that can be paralleled in the Ardagh Chalice *(p70)*. The discs can be compared to glass studs found at the Lagore crannog in County Meath and at other sites.[66] They contain several stylised stepped crosses. Interlace flourishes are placed at each corner of the frame. The borders contain beasts with biting snouts, the outer and the inner panels top and tail corresponding with but not mirroring each other. The creatures in the inner panels resemble reptiles, though with attenuated legs. They take on a C-shape, with some similarity to the animals on the Sutton Hoo purse *(below)*, while the outer panels contain quadrupeds whose snake-like bodies have roughly an S-shape. The single rows of quadrupeds — or so they must be assumed to be, though only two legs are shown — in the side panels process up (on the right) and down

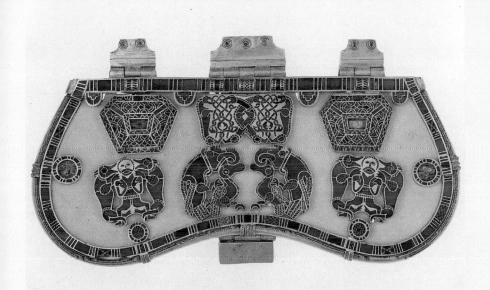

(on the left). They resemble stylistically, though not in a precise way, the beasts of the Durham Gospels folio 2r, a Pictish beast from Golspie, Sutherland, and animals on the Sutton Hoo purse lid and around the edges of one of the pairs of gold shoulder clasps from the same site.[67] In its use of the cross, medallion and a double border, the page is reminiscent of an early Christian funerary slab in the British Museum *(p73)*. Number symbolism can be demonstrated for folio 192v. The two vertical side panels contain three linked beasts (the Trinity), the inner horizontal panels contain eight (the eighth day being the day of Resurrection), and the outer panel contains ten

Sutton Hoo purse lid
(British Museum)

iudaeis sum gens tuae pontifices
tradiderunt mihi quid fecisti
Respondit ihs regnum meum non est
de mundo hoc si ex hoc mundo esset
regnum meum ministri mei decerta
rent utrum non traderer iudaeis nunc
autem meum regnum non est hic ,
DIXIT itaque ei pilatus ergo rex
es tu respondit ihs tu dicis quia rex
sum ego ꞈ EGO in hoc natus sum et
ad hoc ueni in mundum ut testimo
nium perhibeam ueritati omnis
qui est ex ueritate audit meam uoce
dicit ei pilatus quid est ueritas et
cum hoc dixisset iterum exiuit ad iudae
et dicit eis ego nullam inuenio in eo
causam ꞏ est autem consuetudo uobis
ut unum dimittam uobis in pascha
uultis ergo dimittam uobis regem
iudaeorum ,
CLAMAuerunt rursum omnes
dicentes non sed barabban
erat autem barabbas latro ,
TUNC ergo adpraehendit pilatus
ihm et flagillauit et milites plec

animals (St Augustine's conception of unity, a perfect number).[68]

Folio 193r *(p65)* is the most lavish Gospel opening in the manuscript. The shaft of the *IN* of *IN PRINCIPIO* takes up the length of the page. The text is given another three levels of size and decoration. The words *PRIN/CIPIO / ERAT*, written in alternating panels of pen and ink ornament and yellow orpiment surrounded by red dots, stretch over three lines; the words *UERBUM ET UER/BUM ERAT AP/UD DEUM ET DEUS* are in a reduced size but are again surrounded by red dots over a further three lines, and the normal text script occupies eight lines in the right corner.

Detail of funerary slab of limestone, with medallion containing a cross carved in relief *(British Museum)*

OPPOSITE:
Book of Durrow
folio 235v

REBINDING *of* 1954

IN 1953, THE BOOK OF KELLS was rebound in Trinity College Library by Roger Powell, the leading bookbinder of his day. When this work was completed, the consideration of the college authorities turned to the Book of Durrow, which was in a state of considerable disarray. The original quiring having been lost, the manuscript had been whip-stitched into artificial gatherings of six leaves each. Between March and July 1954, the book was extensively repaired and rebound by Roger Powell at the British Museum in London. Due to its status as a national treasure, the college felt it prudent to gain the approval of the Taoiseach, Éamon de Valera, before the manuscript left the country.[69]

Powell disbound the manuscript, cleaned and flattened the leaves through gentle hydration and tensioning, and removed the many patches which a previous binder had placed over holes in the vellum. As he worked, he communicated his findings on the physical structure of the manuscript to A A Luce, editor of the commentary volume to the 1960 facsimile. By March 1954, Luce felt confident that he had solved the problem of where the leaves should be placed in the reconstructed codex, and wrote excitedly to the vice-provost, H W Parke, 'Please keep the foliation to yourself, or we shall have the Irish Times down on us'.[70] Powell observed that the book was written on calfskin vellum which, like the Book of Kells, was variable in texture and colour and was made up in highly irregular gathering sizes. The

OPPOSITE:
Book of Durrow
folio 246r

...ican & quinonha
bet uendat tunica
& emat gladium

Vbi in monte so
lit oracis & dixit
discipulis onate ne
intretis intemptag
onem

& dixit iudae
o sculo filium homi
nis tradis

& dixerunt ad ihm
principes sacerdo
tum sit ues xps dic
nobis & obtulerunt
eum pilato & herodi

& inpassione orat
ihs pater dimitte il
lis quia nesciunt &
in delatronibus di
cit hodie mecum eris
in paradiso

Post resurrectione
apparuit ihs duo
bus euntib: additam
& apostolis & benedi
cens eos ascendit in cae
lis

Johannis
testimonium
perhibet de xpo

dicens non sum dignus
corrigiam calciamen
ti eius soluere

Item iohannes dicit
ecce agnus di qui tol
lit peccata mundi

& ostendit ihs disci
pulis suis ubi manebat
& secuti sunt eum

Ubi ihs de aqua uinu
fecit in channa
galileae

& eiecit ihs de templo
omnes uendentes &
dixit domus oracionis
est domus patris mei

Qui non renatus fue
rit denuo ex aqua
& spu sco non intrabit
in regnum di

Ubi baptizabit ihs
& dicit iohannis
discipulis ego non sum
xps

Ubi saccessit ihs
...iudaea & ue
nit in samariam

Redeut super puteu
cum muliere sa
maritana petit
bibere & dicit dis
cipulis suis

artist normally chose the flesh side of the skin for carpet pages and pages at the opening of Gospels, but used the hair side for three of the symbols, the Man, the Eagle and the Calf. A pronounced follicle pattern can be seen on many pages. Towards the end of the book are several pages using large patches of contemporary vellum written over by the scribe. Powell suggested that vellum may have become scarce by then, and the monks were finding it hard to finish the book. It may however be observed that this practice also occurred towards the beginning of the manuscript, while in other places, such as folio 121r *(p53)*, the scribe wrote around holes in the vellum, ringing the holes with red dots, a practice also observable in the Echternach Gospels.

Powell created bifolia by means of strips of new vellum and bound the book in artificial gatherings of eight. He obtained vellum from Elzas and Zonen, Celbridge, County Kildare and from the English maker H Band; quarter-cut English oak for the boards; and alum-tawed pigskin on the spine from the Gryfe Tannery, Bridge of Weir, Scotland. He estimated that the rebinding involved 150 yards (137 metres) of linen thread and around fifty thousand hand stitches. Refoliation, necessary once the leaves were rearranged, was carried out by a member of the British Museum staff. This can be seen in the top right corner of each leaf.[71]

PIGMENTS
and
INK

THE BOOK OF DURROW employed a narrow palette of colours: a green from verdigris (copper acetate), an orange-red produced from red lead, a yellow from orpiment (yellow arsenic sulphide), whose name in Latin, *auripigmentum* (gold pigment), indicates its use as a substitute for gold. Some use was made of yellow from ox-gall, which tended to discolour to brown. Green, generally absent from the initial pages, is prominent in the symbols and carpet pages, though its effect is less striking now than it must have been when the manuscript was new, as the verdigris has reacted to the wetting of the leaves, leaving areas first of darkening then of perforation of the vellum. Some oxidation and darkening of the red can be observed in places adjacent to the yellow orpiment, for example on 84r, a characteristic chemical reaction. Roosen-Runge observed differences in the quality of the orpiment between, for example, its firm adherence to the vellum on 191v *(p62)*, and its flaking on 86r *(p49)*. This may however be the result not of 'technical defect', as he judged it, but of the harsh treatment that the manuscript has suffered. Like the Macregol Gospel book from Birr (Oxford, Bodleian Library, MS Auct. D. 2. 19), Durrow's artistry is of a kind that cannot always be appreciated in black and white reproduction. Striking colouristic effects are achieved through the skilful balance and switching of the colours in single strands of interlace. In several places, red dotting has been placed over the ink of initial letters of sections. The dotting can be

FOLLOWING PAGES:
Book of Durrow
folios 247v, 248r

77

nor occidentr pri
cept obsequium
o parcene causaba
habebatur sed icenim
uiclebouor extende
bit conuescenum

Etdicebat o discipulis
christi p atendam
prosperum iuram

Pater sce seruacor
ippo mineuio io
esto discipulo

Etdicenum ahin ad
annam etcaipa
etacdiscipilicatum

Etdicenure christihs
discipulo quem
diligebat ecce
materuia

Post Resurrecti on
em apparuit
ihs discipulis et
nonenedebat
thomas ettenui
apparuittei in
cenepateum ᵇᵃ

Etcuntertio mani
festauetse ihs
discipilis et
xpacimo di

ensah poste outine
sr exsaequiuerue
Regio beteuidinem
tuam tepraeuerbicos
pecquei urquicumque
hunctibellummanure
ruerut meminerit celam
bas saespspsosipsqui hecspsi
ni urr euangelium scribere
dierum spacium ...

Ora p nome sna
tcimi clascicum
sit ·

observed, for example, on the *U* of *Uae* on folio 158r *(p60)*, though on most pages it is no longer readily visible because of abrasion. The text of the Book of Durrow was written using an iron-gall ink, mainly brown, but occasionally merging to a blacker shade.[72]

PRINCIPLES OF DESIGN and TIMESCALE OF PRODUCTION

COMPASSES AND A STRAIGHT-EDGE were the artist's basic tools. Unlike the Lindisfarne Gospels, no evidence of ruling lines or puncture marks from dividers is visible to prove this in Durrow, which may be due to the thickness of the pigment, or to the possibility, as Robert Stevick inferred, that the designs were first worked out on separate sheets and then transferred to the book. Stevick identified punctures at the corners of the framing lines of 21v *(p34)* to support this conclusion. On the basis of a study of the Evangelist pages, he concluded that although the borders of the pages were all different, their proportions were worked out according to a formula which derived from the height of the border. The formula broke down to some extent for the Luke symbol page, 124v *(p56)*.[73]

The calligrapher Mark van Stone, who has referred to the 'striking simplicity' of the principles underlying the design of the pages, has expressed a view on the relative difficulties involved in the interlace borders of the

Evangelist pages. The frame round 21v *(p34)* was most difficult to design. In 191v *(p62)*, the borders at top and tail are of the same kind, while those left and right are formed from a Coptic style of interlace which is more easily executed. 'On the frames of the Calf and the Eagle his knots are progressively easier to execute, and the interlace round the Eagle actually mimics the circular knots of the more difficult knotwork around Matthew.' He notes further that some of the interlace was not a complete success. For example, in 124v *(p56)*, the tail border has two rows of ten knots, or 'tulips', as he terms them, while the corresponding top border contains nine knots and one half-knot, a 'degenerate tulip'.[74]

Further analysis of the geometry behind the designs has been advanced by Jacques Guilmain from examination of a leaf which Nordenfalk believed to have come from a pattern book and which is now bound with a manuscript from Corbie in northern France, a monastery with strong insular connections (Paris, Bibliothèque Nationale, lat. 12190, folio Av). Guilmain has provided a reconstruction of Durrow 1v *(p10)*, based on the resemblance of its top and bottom panels to one of the panels of this page.[75]

The inscription on folio 247v *(p78)* claims that the Book of Durrow was written in twelve days. This seems impossible. The legend that the scribe Dimma completed a copy of the Gospels for St Cronan (died 619) in forty days may be closer to the truth, to judge from the experience of the calligrapher Timothy O'Neill. A page of text from the Book of Durrow was copied by him on paper (smoother and probably faster than vellum) in thirty minutes. From this he calculated that the text — though not including the decorated pages — could have been completed in sixty days if the scribe worked for six hours every day in optimum conditions of light and temperature.[76]

bifolium (pl. bifolia)   sheet of writing material folded in half to produce two leaves.

boss   raised or protruding ornament, normally round.

carpet pages   pages of decoration without text.

cloisonné   decorative technique in metalwork in which the colours are separated by thin strips of metal.

colophon   inscription recording the circumstances of production or details of a text or book.

Coptic   pertaining to the Copts, or people of Egypt. In the Middle Ages, the Coptic church was distinctive in some respects from other Christian churches.

crannog   dwelling on an artificial island (from the Irish *crann* = tree)

escutcheon   applied to hanging-bowls, the plate to which the suspension hooks are attached.

filigree   ornament formed from the soldering of wires.

majuscule   a term used to distinguish the higher grade script of the insular period (sixth to ninth centuries) from minuscule, the lower grade.

millefiori   ornament placed in enamel or metalwork. Made by fusing sticks of coloured glass and cutting them into sections.

quire   gatherings of leaves (singles or bifolia or collections of each) from which a book is formed.

Vulgate   Bible in Latin compiled by St Jerome at the command of Pope Damasus (AD 382)

Ir–IIr	*Blank*
IIv	Inscription from the *cumdach* (shrine), with notes and transcription by Roderick O'Flaherty, 1677
IIIr/v	*Blank*
1r	*Blank*
1v	Cross carpet page
2r	Four symbols arranged around a cross
2v–3r	*Blank*
3v	Trumpet and spirals carpet page
4r–6v	[St Jerome's letter to Pope Damasus, beginning] *Nouum Opus*
6v–7v	Interpretations of Hebrew names in St Matthew's Gospel
8r–10r	Eusebian canon tables
8r	Canon I (sections common to all four Gospels)
8v–9r	Canon II (sections common to Matthew, Mark and Luke)
9r	Conclusion of Canon II
	Canon III (sections common to Matthew, Luke and John)
	Canon IV (sections common to Matthew, Mark and John)
9v	Canon V (sections common to Matthew and Luke)
	Canon VI (sections common to Matthew and Mark)
	Canon VII (sections common to Matthew and John)
	Canon VIII (sections common to Luke and Mark)
10r	Canon IX (sections common to Luke and John)
	Canon X (sections peculiar to Matthew, Mark, Luke and John respectively)
10v	*Blank*
11r–14rᵃ	*Breues causae* of St Matthew
14rᵇ 15rᵃ	*Argumentum* of St Matthew
15rᵇ–17rᵃ	*Breues causae* of St Mark
17rᵇ–18rᵃ	*Argumentum* of St Mark
18rᵇ–19vᵃ	*Argumentum* of St Luke
19vᵇ–20vᵃ	*Argumentum* of St John
20vᵇ	Interpretations of Hebrew names in Gospels of St John and St Mark
21r	*Blank*

21v	The Man, symbol of St Matthew
22r–84r	St Matthew's Gospel
84v	The Eagle, symbol of St Mark
85r	*Blank*
85v	Carpet page with roundels
86r–123v	St Mark's Gospel
124r	Interpretations of Hebrew names in Gospel of St Luke
124v	The Calf, symbol of St Luke. Also contains a note by Conall Mac Eochagáin, asking for a blessing on his soul, Christmas Day 1633.[77]
125r	*Blank*
125v	Carpet page
126r–191r	St Luke's Gospel
191r	'Neamanus.' An inscription at the foot of the page reads: + miserere dñe naemání + + flii. nech⁻ + Luce translated this as 'have mercy, O Lord, on Neamanus, son of Nechtan', and reported Charles O'Conor's identification of the subject with a late-fifteenth-century figure, Naemanus O'Donnel.[78] Dáibhí Ó Cróinín has suggested that the name should be read 'N. mac nEchach', that is N. son of Eochu, a figure who may perhaps be identified with Némán mac Echdach of the genealogies, who may be placed in the early seventh century and was a distant relative of St Colum Cille.[79]
191v	The Lion, symbol of St John
192r	*Originally blank.* Acts 2. 1–4 added in eleventh or twelfth century
192v	Carpet page with central cross and biting animals in borders
193r–242r	St John's Gospel
242v–246r	*Breues causae* of St Luke
246r–247v	*Breues causae* of St John
247v[b]	Colophons
248r	Carpet page with 'lattice' work
248v	Record of a legal transaction concerning the abbey of Durrow, added in eleventh century

Old Library, Trinity College Dublin, *c* 1830 to date[80]

Treasures of Trinity College, Dublin
Royal Academy, London (January to March 1961)[81]

Treasures of Early Irish Art
Metropolitan Museum of Art, New York (October 1977 to January 1978)
Fine Arts Museums of San Francisco, de Young Memorial Museum (February to May 1978)
Museum of Art, Carnegie Institute, Pittsburgh (June to September 1978)
Museum of Fine Arts, Boston (October 1978 to January 1979)
Philadelphia Museum of Art (February to May 1979)
National Museum of Ireland, Dublin (May 1980 to November 1981)[82]

Treasures of Ireland
Grand Palais, Paris (October 1982 to January 1983)
Wallraf-Richartz Museum, Köln (February to May 1983)
Staatliche Museen Preußischer Kulturbesitz, Berlin (June to October 1983)
Rijksmuseum, Amsterdam (November 1983 to February 1984)
Louisiana Museum, Humlebæk, near Copenhagen (March to June 1984)[83]

NOTES

1. The term 'insular' is commonly used as a neutral term, one which avoids national specifics, to describe the style of art and script used in Britain and Ireland in the period between the sixth and ninth centuries.

2. Adomnán, p7.

3. Bede, *HE*, pp222–3.

4. Adomnán, pp25, 57, 203, 97.

5. Bede, *HE*, pp222–3.

6. Peter Harbison, *The High Crosses of Ireland. An Iconographical and Photographic Survey*, 3 vols (Bonn 1992), vol 1, pp79–83, 367–71.

7. Luce et al (1960), pp17–24, 32.

8. Bernard Meehan, *The Book of Kells. An Illustrated Introduction to the Manuscript in Trinity College Dublin* (London 1994), pp14, 94, n5.

9. Transcripts of such agreements were commonly written into Gospel books for reasons of permanence and safekeeping: see G Mac Niocaill in *Kells commentary*, p153; R I Best, 'An Early Monastic Grant in the Book of Durrow', *Ériu*, 10 (1926–8), pp135–42; Luce et al (1960), p30.

10 *The Whole Works of the Most Rev James Ussher, DD*, ed C R Elrington (Dublin 1847–64), 17 vols, vol 6, p232. For the date 1623, see William O'Sullivan, 'Correspondence of David Rothe and James Ussher, 1619–23', *Collectanea Hibernica* 36–37 (1994–5), pp7–49.

11. Luce et al (1960), p66.

12. Bernard Meehan, 'Elements of Manuscript Production in the Middle Ages', *The Illustrated Archaeology of Ireland*, ed Michael Ryan (Dublin 1991), pp139–43, at p143.

13. Luce et al (1960), p66

14. Powell (1956), pp14–15.

15. William O'Sullivan, 'The Donor of the Book of Kells', *Irish Historical Studies* 11 (1958–9), pp5–7; Luce et al (1960), pp78–9.

16. Quoted in Luce et al (1960), p53.

17. R N Bailey, 'Sutton Hoo and Seventh-Century Art', in *Sutton Hoo: Fifty Years After*, ed R Farrell and C Neumann de Vegvar. *American Early Medieval Studies* 2 (1992), pp31–41.

18. CLA 2, pp xiv–xv.

19. Nordenfalk (1947), p174.

20. T J Brown, 'Northumbria and the Book of Kells', *A Palaeographer's View: Selected Writings of Julian Brown*, ed J Bately, M Brown, J Roberts (London 1993), pp97–124. For a synopsis of the debate, see ibid, pp98–102.

21. CLA 2 (2nd edn), p43.

22. Nordenfalk (1947), p171, n 39

23. *A Palaeographer's View*, p208.

24. *Irish Art in the Early Christian Period to 800 AD* (London 1965), p173. For dating of the Carndonagh and Fahan Mura sculptures, see Harbison (1992), pp375–6.

25. Luce et al, p53.

26. Dáibhí Ó Cróinín, 'Pride and Prejudice', *Peritia* 1 (1982), pp352–62; 'Rath Melsigi, Willibrord, and the Earliest Echternach Manuscripts', *Peritia* 3 (1984), pp17–49; 'Is the Augsburg Gospel Codex a Northumbrian Manuscript?', *St Cuthbert, his Cult and Community to A.D. 1200*, ed G Bonner, C Stancliffe and D Rollason (Woodbridge, 1989), pp189–201. See also a review of the controversy by Nordenfalk in *Ireland and Insular Art*, pp1–6.

27. Henderson, p55.

28. *Kells conference Proceedings* (1994), p486.

29. See Alexander (1978), pp80–81, plates 277–280.

30. William O'Sullivan, 'The Lindisfarne Scriptorium: For and Against', *Peritia* 8 (1994), pp80–94, at p85. See also his 'Insular Calligraphy: Current State and Problems', *Peritia* 4 (1985), pp346–359, at pp353–4.

31. *Irish Art in the Early Christian Period to 800 AD* (London 1965), p169.

32. Ernst Kitzinger, 'Interlace and Icons: Form and Function in Early Insular Art', *Age of Migrating Ideas*, pp3–15.

33. Alexander (1978), p28 and plate 6.

34. Other instances may be cited of colophons copied from earlier manuscripts, such as the Mulling inscription in Trinity College Dublin, MS 60: see Bernard Meehan, 'Book of Mulling', in *Space in European Art. Council of Europe Exhibition in Japan* (The National Museum of Western Art, Tokyo, 1987), pp103–4.

35. P McGurk, *Kells commentary* (1990), pp52–7.

36. Powell (1956).

37. See *Kells commentary* (1990), p47.

38. J Chapman, *Notes on the Early History of the Vulgate Gospels* (Oxford 1908). The *Breues causae* and *Argumenta* follow an unusual order, one which again is found in the Book of Kells.

39. Luce et al, p84.

40. Werner (1984–6), pp6–7. See also R E McNally, 'The Evangelists in the Hiberno-Latin Tradition', in *Festschrift Bernhard Bischoff*, ed J Autenrieth and F Brunhölz (Stuttgart 1971), pp111–122.

41. *Kells conference Proceedings* (1994), p455.

42. Raghnall Ó Floinn, *Irish Shrines and Reliquaries of the Middle Ages* (Dublin 1994), pp37–9. See also a late twelfth-century German or Italian reliquary cross now in the Cleveland Museum of Art: *Memory and the Middle Ages*, exhibition catalogue February 17–May 21, 1995, ed N Netzer and V Reinburg (Boston College Museum of Art 1995), p26, no 20.

43. Werner (1990), fig 7.

44. P Harbison, 'The Antrim Cross in the Hunt Museum', *North Munster Antiquarian Journal* 20 (1978), pp17–40; Haseloff, p191.

45. Werner (1990).

46. J O Westwood, *Palaeographia sacra pictoria* (1843), 'Irish Biblical MSS, plate II', p2.

47. Meyer was mistaken in indicating feet: Luce et al (1960), p103.

48. Haseloff, p101, central figures; p159.

49. Henderson (1987), p20; *The Work of Angels. Masterpieces of Celtic Metalwork, 6th to 9th Centuries AD* (London 1989), p66.

50. Ibid, p41.

51. F Henry, *Irish Art in the Early Christian Period to 800 AD* (London 1965), pl 50; Alexander, fig 8.

52. Harbison (1992), fig 88.

53. Reproduced in colour in *Minerva* (Nov/Dec 94), p29.

54. *Irish Art in the Early Christian Period to 800 AD* (London 1965), pls 54–55.

55. Meehan, *Book of Kells* (1994), p21, pl 18.

56. Niamh Whitfield, 'Formal Conventions in the Depiction of Animals on Celtic Metalwork', figs 10.10–11, *Third Insular Art Conference*, ed Cormac Bourke (forthcoming, Belfast 1995).

57. Reproduced in *Wealth of the Roman World AD 300–700*, ed J P C Kent and K S Painter (London 1977), pp156–7, no 329. See also W O'Sullivan in *Peritia* 8, p89.

58. Alexander (1978), pl 226

59. Carl Nordenfalk, *Celtic and Anglo-Saxon Painting* (New York 1977), p43.

60. Henderson (1987), pl 27.

61. Alexander (1978), fig 8.

62. C Thomas, 'A Black Cat among the Pictish Beasts', *Pictish Arts Society Journal* 6 (1994) pp1–8, fig v.

63. *Age of Migrating Ideas*, pp19–20.

64. Alexander (1978), pl 114.

65. Reproduced in W Gillon, *A Short History of African Art* (Viking 1984), p226, pl 157.

66. Haseloff, pp180, 183, 187–8.

67. *Age of Migrating Ideas*, p21. A C Evans, *The Sutton Hoo Ship Burial* (London 1986), pl vi. For drawings of the animals, see Eva Wilson, *Early Medieval Designs from Britain*. British Museum Pattern Books (London 1983), figs 30, 31.

68. Carola Hicks, *Animals in Early Medieval Art* (Edinburgh 1993), pp87–9; H Richardson in *Journal of the Royal Society of Antiquaries of Ireland* 114 (1984), pp28–47.

69. For a similar sensitivity concerning the rebinding of the Book of Kells, see *Kells commentary* (1990), p194.

70. Library correspondence.

71. Powell (1956).

72. Robert Fuchs and Doris Oltrogge, 'Colour Material and Painting Technique in the Book of Kells', *Kells conference Proceedings* (1994), pp133–171, at pp170–1; Roosen-Runge in *Evangeliorum quattuor codex Lindisfarnensis*, ed T D Kendrick et al (Olten, Lausanne, 1956–60), vol 2, p273.

73. Stevick (1986), pp192–3, fig 11. See also Stevick (1994).

74. Note *Kells conference Proceedings* (1994), pp234–5, 241.

75. Jacques Guilmain, 'An Analysis of some Ornamental Patterns in Hiberno-Saxon Manuscript Illumination in Relation to their Mediterranean Origins', *Age of Migrating Ideas*, pp92–103. For the construction of this page, see p98. A colour plate of the Paris manuscript is in G Bologna, *Illuminated Manuscripts: the Book before Gutenberg* (London 1988).

76. Bernard Meehan, 'Irish Manuscripts in the Early Middle Ages', in *Treasures of Ireland. Irish Art 3000 BC – 1500 AD* (Dublin 1983), pp48–55, at p48; Timothy O'Neill, 'Book-making in Early Christian Ireland', *Archaeology Ireland* 3 (1989), pp96–100, at p99.

77. Luce et al (1960), p67.

78. Luce et al (1960), p31.

79. *Corpus genealogiarum Hiberniae* 1, ed M A O'Brien (Dublin 1962, reprinted 1976), p165. I am very grateful to Dr Ó Cróinín for sight of his unpublished paper, 'The "Nemanus" inscription in the Book of Durrow'.

80. *Kells commentary* (1990), p324.

81. *Treasures of Trinity College, Dublin: An exhibition chosen from the college and its library at Burlington House, London, W1*, 12 January–March 1961, compiled by F J E Hurst (London 1961).

82. *Treasures of Early Irish Art 1500 BC to 1500 AD, from the collections of the National Museum of Ireland, Royal Irish Academy, Trinity College Dublin* (New York: The Metropolitan Museum of Art 1977).

83. *Treasures of Ireland: Irish Art 3000 BC–1500 AD* (Dublin 1983), and bibliography.

SELECT BIBLIOGRAPHY AND ABBREVIATIONS

Adomnán (1991)
Adomnán's Life of Columba, ed A O and M O Anderson, revised edn (Oxford 1991)

Age of Migrating Ideas (1993)
The Age of Migrating Ideas. Early Medieval Art in Northern Britain and Ireland, ed R Michael Spearman and John Higgitt (Edinburgh 1993)

Alexander (1978)
J J G Alexander, *Insular Manuscripts, 6th to the 9th Century*, A survey of manuscripts illuminated in the British Isles 1 (London 1978), pp30–32, plates 11–22

Bede, *HE*
Bede's Ecclesiastical History of the English People, ed B Colgrave and R A B Mynors (Oxford 1969)

CLA
Codices latini antiquiores: a palaeographical guide to Latin manuscripts prior to the ninth century, ed E A Lowe I–XI, Suppl (1934–72)

Marvin L Colker, with an introduction by William O'Sullivan, *Trinity College Library Dublin. Descriptive Catalogue of the Mediaeval and Renaissance Latin Manuscripts* (Aldershot: Scolar Press, for Trinity College Library Dublin, 1991), vol 1, pp104–6

Haseloff (1990)
Gunther Haseloff, *Email im frühen Mittelalter. Frühchristliche Kunst von der Spätantike bis zu den Karolingern* (Marburg 1990)

Henderson (1987)
George Henderson, *From Durrow to Kells. The Insular Gospel-books 650–800* (London 1987)

Ireland and Insular Art
Ireland and Insular Art AD 500–1200, ed Michael Ryan (Dublin 1987)

Kells commentary (1990)
The Book of Kells, MS 58, Trinity College Library Dublin: Commentary, ed Peter Fox (Faksimile Verlag Luzern 1990)

Kells conference Proceedings (1994)
The Book of Kells. Proceedings of a Conference at Trinity College Dublin, 6–9 September 1992, ed Felicity O'Mahony (Aldershot: Scolar Press, for Trinity College Library, Dublin 1994)

Luce et al (1960)
Evangeliorum Quattuor Codex Durmachensis, facsimile of Book of Durrow, 2 volumes (Olten, Lausanne, 1960), with introductory matter: 'Editor's introduction' by A A Luce; 'The palaeography of the Book of Durrow' by L Bieler; 'The art of the Book of Durrow' by P Meyer; 'The text of Codex Durmachensis collated with the text of Codex Amiatinus together with an inventory or summary description of the contents of each page of the manuscript' by G O Simms.

Nordenfalk (1947)
Carl Nordenfalk, 'Before the Book of Durrow', *Acta Archaeologica* 18 (1947), pp141–74

Nordenfalk (1968)
Carl Nordenfalk, 'An Illustrated Diatessaron', *Art Bulletin* 50 (1968), pp119–40

Nordenfalk (1973)
Carl Nordenfalk, 'The Persian Diatessaron Once Again', *Art Bulletin* 55 (1973), pp532–46

Powell (1956)
Roger Powell, 'The Book of Kells, the Book of Durrow. Notes on the Vellum, the Make-up, and other Aspects', *Scriptorium* 10 (1956), pp3–21

Stevick (1986)
Robert D Stevick, 'The Shapes of the Book of Durrow Evangelist-Symbol Pages', *The Art Bulletin* 68 (1986), pp182–194

Stevick (1994)
The Earliest Irish and English Bookarts. Visual and Poetic Forms before AD 1000 (Philadelphia 1994)

Werner (1984–86)
Martin Werner, 'On the Origin of Zoanthropomorphic Evangelist Symbols: the Early Christian Background', *Studies in Iconography* 10 (1984–86), pp1–35

Werner (1990)
Martin Werner, 'The Cross-Carpet Page in the Book of Durrow: The Cult of the True Cross, Adomnán, and Iona', *The Art Bulletin* 72 (1990), pp174–223

Werner (1994)
Martin Werner, 'Crucifixi, Sepulti, Suscitati: Remarks on the Decoration of the Book of Kells', *Kells conference Proceedings* (1994)

Zimmermann
E H Zimmermann, *Vorkarolingische Miniaturen* I–IV (Berlin 1916–18)

Schmidt